AULD ACQUAINTANCE

AULD ACQUAINTANCE

Great Scots Characters I Have Known

BEN COUTTS

THE MERCAT PRESS
EDINBURGH

First published in 1994 by Mercat Press
James Thin, 53 South Bridge, Edinburgh EH1 1YS

ISBN 1873644 302

Typeset by Hewer Text Composition Services Ltd, Edinburgh

Printed in Great Britain by
The Cromwell Press, Melksham

Contents

Illustrations

Acknowledgements

Firstly, as always, my long-suffering wife Sal, who has had to spend all too much time during our recent holidays walking along the cliffs or on the beaches (or reading *Wild Swans*, which luckily took up quite a bit of her time) while I scribbled. Sadly, being completely unmechanically minded I haven't even managed to master a typewriter, never mind a word processor, so I have had to rely on Isobel Johnston, a nice neighbour, to decipher my awful scrawl and deliver to me not one, but two, beautifully typed copies of each chapter with hardly one mistake, incredible. Then, to all those who were related or knew well one of my 'characters' and either lent me a photo or told me a story about them, my thanks. As someone who loves a 'tellin' of the tale', as the Irish say, I hope I haven't overstepped the mark, but if I have, my apologies. One or two who weren't able to help me (though I asked them) with their reminiscences about characters no longer with us can't blame me if I haven't done them justice! Acknowledgements too to Professor Tim Cox of Cambridge and Dr Morrison of Crieff who have kept me in the 'breathing business'. Also to Ainslie Thin and his henchmen Tom Johnstone and Seán Costello, who think these ramblings of mine are worth printing (I hope they are right).

And finally, my gratitude to Bacchus, god of wine, as without him not a word would have been written – the stuff that 'gladdens the heart of man', as the old book says, also does wonders to the flow of ink as well as helping 'memory hold the door'.

To all, my sincere thanks.

HER MAJESTY, QUEEN ELIZABETH THE QUEEN MOTHER

Scotland's greatest character

Although the Popular Press have done their best over the last few years to denigrate the Monarchy and the Royal Family generally, one person has stood out head and shoulders, perhaps not in stature, but by her behaviour, above anything they have tried to do, and that person has been the Queen Mother. She must be the most looked up to and loved lady in the land, and rightly so, as she has always behaved impeccably and has a wonderful way of dealing with the press, photographers and the people I call 'the Jocks', the ordinary people who do the ordinary jobs in this country of ours. Be it the stocksmen, with whom she is completely at home, the bumarees at Smithfield Market, the jockeys at a National Hunt meeting, you name them, I'll bet she'll get on with them and be able to talk knowledgeably about the job they do. I read a review the other day of a book written about the Queen Mother and it said 'the usual saccharine stuff '. Dear reviewer, 'jealousy will get you nowhere'. Once you've been fortunate to meet this gracious lady and had those piercing blue eyes fixed on you it would only be a fool who wouldn't realise what a wonderful person we have had to lead the Royal Family for all these years. Oh! I know it's all very well saying that some of the young haven't lived up to their calling, but every family nowadays has problems, and most don't have the popular press following them day and night in order to get a 'scoop'!

I was fortunate some twenty-two years ago to be invited to the Castle of Mey for lunch. The reason for the invitation arose from the fact that I was Secretary of the Aberdeen-Angus Cattle Society. My then President said to me that as the Hereford Cattle Society had Antony Eden as their patron, and were using him and his name at every possible opportunity, what were we doing about ours, who was the Queen Mother? The answer was simply all too little, as apart from opening the new offices in Perth, Her Majesty had never been approached by anyone, nor had her cattle been seen at any time. As luck would have it her Personal Secretary was Sir Martin Gilliatt, who had worked with brother Wally in Kenya, so I wrote to him asking if it would be possible to go to see the Queen Mother's herd, little realising I was to be asked to the first of many happy lunches with Her Majesty.

That first one was fraught with problems, firstly because I decided to fly from Aberdeen to Wick where I was to be picked up by an Aberdeen-Angus breeder and taken to Mey. Imagine my consternation when I arrived at Aberdeen to be told that because of fog at Heathrow (and it was a wonderful clear day in Aberdeen), there would be no plane to go on to Wick. Talk about panic stations! An invitation to lunch with the Queen Mum and here I was stranded in Aberdeen. I went to the person in charge of the Airport, which wasn't as big then as it is today, and explained my predicament. He, luckily, like most of us, was a great admirer of Her Majesty and said, 'I'll get you a chap who flies taxis'. He wasn't to know the poor fellow had one helluva hangover and nearly crash-landed us at Wick as he didn't remember to put his wheels down until he got a message from the ground. Either he was embarrassed about that incident or he was such a dedicated Royalist, I know not, but I never got a bill for that flight!

The next thing was that, after the initial introductions were over, and at the thought of it even now after all these years I feel a tingle of nerves, I was told it was a larger lunch party than usual, as her Estate Factor was retiring – to be replaced, might I say, by someone whom I had known for many years and who is still there doing a sterling job, one Martin Leslie.

I was sat on Her Majesty's left, with her retiring Factor on her right, and she said, 'I'm afraid I won't be saying much to you at lunch because I wish to talk to my Factor'. Despite this, it amazed me then, and still does, how much homework the Royals put in with regard to their guests, as Her Majesty knew I was factoring Blackmount for the Fleming family and she used to invite Peter Fleming and his wife Celia Johnson to Windsor for weekends. The only questions Her Majesty asked me during that lunch were to do with Blackmount.

I had on my left Lady Ruth Fermoy, a lovely person in every way, who must now be sorely missed by the Queen Mum. It was hard indeed that she should have two of her best friends and confidantes taken in one year, as Sir Martin Gilliatt and Lady Ruth died at the same time. Not only was Lady Ruth excellent company but the steward, whom I've got to know over the years, knew instinctively that I appreciated good wine and was more than liberal in dispensing it to me.

Imagine my complete surprise when Her Majesty got up and asked her relation, the Earl of Strathmore of Glamis, who was sitting at the other end of the table, to take over, as her gardener, Sinclair, wanted to show Captain Coutts the potatoes that Captain Coutts had recommended in one of his

The Queen Mother

Two Vice-Presidents of the Royal Smithfield Club — Her Majesty the Queen Mother and the author — meet at the annual show, Earls Court, 1984. On the right with catalogue, Denis Emus A.F.C., Chairman that year, and on his right Earl Ferrers, now Minister of State at the Home Office

farming broadcasts. We went downstairs. The Castle of Mey is a super building, compact and with naturally good taste in every room, but giving one the feeling of warmth and of being lived in and loved by its owner. At the bottom of the stairs is a small 'loo' in which Her Majesty had her corgis, and on that occasion a certain one called, I think, 'Robbie' didn't like me. Her Majesty assured me his lunge at my ankle was only him being playful – but it felt more like a nip to me!!

It was a terrible day, but one of the Queen Mother's strengths, and my goodness hasn't she plenty, is that she has always taken physical exercise. The number of times I've been at Mey and thought how nice it would be to go for a snooze, only to be told to be ready for a walk along the cliffs or around the gardens. And how right Her Majesty has been to keep active, when one sees what she can do at ninety three! On this first occasion it was blowing a gale force eight or nine (it always seems to be that in Caithness!) and there was plenty of rain in the wind too, but nothing daunted, Her Majesty donned her sou-wester and her oilskin and set off for the garden that, because of the winds, is walled all round. Once we got there, Sinclair showed me my four favourite varieties of tatties, Sharpe's Express, Duke of York's, Kerr's Pink and Golden Wonder, to be eaten in that order.

It was on that first visit to the Castle of Mey when it was coming down whole water and blowing a force nine gale that Her Majesty agreed with me that each country had its 'tipple', and that it was no wonder Scotland's was whisky, though sadly some took too much. (Thinking of the excellent lunch of which I had just partaken I was including myself!) I went on to say that in the awful climate of the West Coast it could be a real problem and was known as 'the weakness'. H.M. laughed and said, 'What a lovely word for it, I must remember it'. The next year when I was invited back to lunch H.M. mentioned Mr X, a mutual acquaintance, and ended, sadly, 'now he has died – of "the weakness"'!

One of the things I've always admired about this great character is her interest in so many subjects worldwide. Before the untimely death of George VI they had done a tremendous amount of travelling and like me had loved it, and certain places naturally more than others. South Africa was a country to which we both had an especial leaning, and we agreed how sad it was that this lovely country, which has everything any country would need, is being torn apart by racial differences, usually fomented by a few. Just this autumn (1993) we both agreed that if anyone suggested a choice of a holiday in the world South Africa would be our number one.

I said at the beginning of this chapter how it annoys me that certain sections of the media harp on about the waste of money the Royal Family are to the public purse etc., etc. I wonder how many people in this country realise that when 'Elizabeth of Glamis' married her beloved 'Bertie' (and my! what a lucky let out we had when 'Teddy' abdicated) they hadn't a roof over their heads and like all other young marrieds had to find accommodation! Changed days indeed, when some of the young Royals are able to build magnificent edifices!

Her Majesty's terrific faith and loyalty to the Church, both the Church of England and the Church of Scotland have meant so much to her, and as a fellow believer I'm sure have had a terrific effect on the whole conduct of her life. I don't know what she usually does in the South, but I know she has been not only a regular attender but a loyal supporter of the ministers at Crathie and Castleton. One of those at Castleton played a guitar and had a very pleasant voice, and after dinner, at which he and I had been guests, Her Majesty asked him to lead us in a sing-song. I remember well 'Glasgow belongs to me' and 'You can't push your Granny off the bus' being sung by everyone with great relish. One of the things I admire most about Her Majesty is that one can be part of a party of that sort after dinner, when everyone is totally relaxed, but next day it's 'on parade, on parade' and 'What have the cattle done since last you saw them, Captain Coutts?' or 'What sort of trade do you think we'll get for these bulls in February?' etc., etc. I think Her Majesty has the wonderful gift of being adaptable, she can get on with the greatest in the land and the lowest in the land, speak to them and understand their problems, and has left many people I know feeling so much better for meeting her and having been spoken to by her. I remember well after Her Majesty had asked me why she had never been invited to attend the Royal Smithfield Club Show, which of course I set in motion right away, the barmaid at the most popular bar in the then Earls Court said, 'Ben, if I could meet the Queen Mum, I'd die happy'. I popped her into a line of cattlemen, and the dear lass had bought a most expensive bouquet of red roses for Her Majesty. But the nice thing is that Her Majesty said to me, 'Get that lady's address, please, and give it to my Lady in Waiting'. Pat Bentley got a letter headed Clarence House, which I know is a very treasured possession. It's just those wee touches of kindness, thoughtfulness and humanity that make this character so special.

Because I was Secretary of the Aberdeen-Angus Society for ten years I had many occasions to meet this gracious Lady, and always after a meeting I came away not only feeling the better for it but admiring the professionalism with which she carried out her job. Her Majesty graced the Society at its centenary lunch which was held in the Elphinstone Hall in Aberdeen – very appropriately, as Elphinstone is of course one of her family names. One of my council, who knew Her Majesty enjoyed a wee gin and Dubonnet 'with plenty of ice' stupidly poured a really strong one. Her Majesty took one sip and never touched another drop; professional as always, as she was due to make and did make a first class speech.

She has a wonderful sense of humour and enjoys a joke. I remember as I was introducing Her Majesty in my speech at that lunch, and knowing her love of fishing, telling about the time she asked her ghillie Sandy, who always wore a deer-stalker bonnet, and as it was a very windy day, 'Why haven't you got your flaps down, Sandy?' To which he replied, 'I've never had them down since my accident'. Her Majesty asked, 'What accident?' and he said, 'the time you offered me a dram and I never heard you'!!!

I had one of the nicest letters I've ever had after that lunch from Her Majesty's Lady in Waiting saying what fun it had all been and how relaxed Her Majesty was – though she had said to me before, 'I wish I hadn't to speak, I'm always so nervous, it's all right for you with all your broadcasting and public speaking'; and I said, as I always do, 'I'm as nervous as the first time I ever made a public speech, and if I wasn't I'd know I was going to be no damned good!'

The 'professionalism' showed again when the Smithfield Club Council were asked to the Castle of Mey. It was arranged that they would hold their annual March meetings in Wick and go out in the afternoon to the Castle to see the North Country Cheviot flock of sheep and the Aberdeen-Angus herd of cattle. There was a phone call during the morning from the Castle to say that transport would call for me before lunch, as Her Majesty wished to discuss the afternoon's programme with me which she would like to do over lunch. It turned out that she wanted me to introduce the members of Council to her, but what happened? Her Majesty knew them all by name as well if not better than I did. Professionalism. Then there was another time at Earls Court, and the usual group of stocksmen and women, barmaids, you name 'em, the sort we felt Her Majesty would like to meet, and at the same time those who had done a good job for the show, were lined up to be presented. There was a very dubious character who looked like 'Mack the Knife' half way down the line and completely unknown to me. The ever faithful John, the private detective, whispered in my ear, 'Do you know that suspicious looking character with the belted-up macintosh, Ben?' When I said a very definite 'No', two 'tecs appeared from nowhere and gave the chap the quickest bum's rush I've ever seen. But the thing that impressed me more than that was the way Her Majesty, never flickering an eyelid, talked a bit longer to the person with whom she was conversing, waited until 'Mack the Knife' was removed, and then moved on down the line. Professionalism.

Then there was the super occasion when Martin Leslie, her Factor, thought up the nice idea that all those who had been associated with the Queen Mother in Caithness would like to mark her ninetieth birthday with something tangible, so he commissioned a well known artist to paint the Castle of Mey, which looks most impressive in the picture with the Firth behind it and Her Majesty's Royal Banner flying and the old black cannons in front. But what really makes the painting something special is that round the margin are depicted all the interests in Caithness that Her Majesty holds most dear: the local Church, her lovely garden, the cliffs on which she walks as often as possible (and having accompanied her on one occasion, complete with corgis, when I say walk I mean walk), then an Angus bull and a North Country Cheviot tup.

As there is not a really big room in the Castle of Mey it was arranged that the presentation should be in the local British Legion Hall, and naturally security was strict, although, thank God, not as visible in Caithness as in London, so we all had passes. One silly ass, whom I knew, brought his girlfriend but not his wife, and got her into the assembled company. After the presentation and speeches the seats were cleared, and with cups of tea and drams in our hands we made a circle in the hall. Accompanied by Martin the gracious lady went round to thank everyone personally for their contribution. That's 'bigness'. But when she came to the chap who had the girlfriend not the wife, she did a nifty half circle and by-passed him. That's Professionalism.

It was lovely this autumn to see not only that picture hanging in the dining room, but also on show on the sideboard the Caithness Glass bowl presented to Her Majesty by the Aberdeen-Angus Society at our Centenary Lunch. On it we had Glamis Castle, Buckingham Palace and Castle of Mey engraved. And the table mats, part of the tastefully set table that adds so much to the Castle of Mey lunches, were the Aberdeen-Angus ones I had given Her Majesty all those twenty-one years ago. All those little touches make one realise what a thoughtful and caring person this special character is.

And talking of being thoughtful, when I was to go to Buck House to receive my M.B.E., Queen Elizabeth asked, through Martin Gilliatt, if the daughters were coming South; and hearing they were, said that she was sorry she wasn't to be at home but she would love them to look around Clarence House if they so wished. I have all my life believed you can sense the sort of person who lives in a house when you enter it. Clarence House has a warmth about it like its resident. There are piles of books and papers (which I'm sure are a headache to those who have to dust them) but every one of the books, magazines, etc. is indexed in the resident's mind. Then there are the family photos, so dear to us all, and in this case one of Prince Charles coming 'out of the plate' (i.e. the saddle) signed 'Charles Jorrocks'!! It was all so homely one could see why the Queen Mother is the lynch-pin of the Royal Family.

And of course there were endless rows of books, including all Dick Francis's, whom I understand goes each year to lunch at Clarence House complete with his latest, suitably signed. To those readers who are not interested in racing, Dick Francis was the Queen Mother's jockey, and rode the ill-fated Devon Loch that looked odds on to win the Grand National for the Queen Mother. It would have been the most popular win for a generation, but suddenly the horse's legs went from him coming up the final straight and that was that. I too love National Hunt racing, which Dad rightly called a 'mug's game', so every time I've been privileged to be with Her Majesty we talk 'osses.

I told her one of Dad's Glasgow stories (he being a Church of Scotland Minister I might say) about the bible-thumping do-gooder woman going down her side street in Glasgow on one of that city's famous murky wet cold days, and seeing a wee 'shilpit' man with his 'hooker-doon' well over his nose, and both bunnet and nose dripping. She pushed some money in his hand and said, 'Never despair, my man', and walked on. A week later the sun was shining, the woman was coming down the same road and the man came racing up to her. He said, 'Here woman, I've been looking for you. Your horse, Never Despair, won at five to one!' He was of course the bookie's runner, one of a well known race in Glasgow before the war, when everyone wanted to make a pile to get out of the awful depression and probably lost what little they had trying to do so.

I was fortunate enough to be part of Her Majesty's party at Cheltenham one year, and how she is adored by the crowd. However, when she speaks of her early days in racing, I think she feels as I do that while of course we need sponsorship, sometimes those who come are more interested in the free beer than the racing. I remember one of the best race meetings I ever attended was in the West of Ireland, I think Sligo, but does it matter? The great Pat Taffe, Arkle's jockey, was riding. The whole thing was what National Hunt is all about, no finesse, no special enclosures, big jumps, good horses, good viewing and the only snag was you couldn't get near the bookies for the priests!!

I always think that racing is a great leveller. There are breeders, owners, trainers, jockeys, bookies, punters – you name them, racing has them – but all depend on horses. We may breed them to gallop or jump better, but at the end of the day they are the deciding factor whether they are to be a Desert Orchid or pull a codger's cart (and I always seem to back the latter). Even the greatest in the land can be ruled by them, as happened when Devon Loch was about to win the National and lost in the last furlong. But what was the Queen Mother's first reaction? Not one of deep, deep annoyance and a wish to blame others, but an immediate word of comfort to both trainer and jockey . That's Bigness.

Yes, and the way Her Majesty treats those whom she calls her 'family' is Bigness. The 'family' includes not only Martin Gilliatt and Ruth Fermoy, whom I knew well and now have sadly passed on, but all of her staff in whatever position. Everyone who serves in the 'family' have told me how much they enjoy working with Her Majesty, because of the way she treats them. That's Bigness. You don't just inherit that gift, you've got to work at it, and Her Majesty has it to a tee.

Quite the most outstanding day I have been honoured to have with the Queen Mother was in July 1992. I was due to have lunch with Martin Gilliatt who had been in hospital, and it was his first day 'out of prison' as he said later. He told me to meet him at Clarence House, but I little realised that I was to be part of a private lunch party, as I thought Martin and I were to have lunch at his club. It was lovely warm sunny day, and we lunched in the Clarence House gardens under the trees. Although it is bang next to the Mall, because of the high wall and hedge one hears nothing. Martin, although obviously not well, told the most lovely stories about the hospital, and how he had to slip down to the local pub to get his favourite pink gin! I little realised it was the last time we would meet. I understand that, as a bachelor, he was taken into Clarence House from his own flat and given the best attention possible until the reaper eventually took his toll. Oh! and I know of many other cases, for example James Fairgrieve, head lad to Peter Cazalet, a Scot who retired to his native country and was allowed to buy a couple of horses for Her Majesty – and one, Earl's Castle, trained by Ken Oliver, won at Ayr in 1973. Yes, Bigness. Maybe she is small in stature but she is big in heart and giving.

In my opinion this country has been lucky to have this Scottish character with so many Scottish characteristics: dependence on a faith, loyalty, honesty, doing a job well (which I have called Professionalism) and thinking of others (which I have called Bigness). But above all these I put the fantastic sense of humour and those blue, blue eyes, that once you've seen them you're hooked. Of course there are bound to be faults, as we all have them, but in this character there is no way that I want to try to find them.

All I can say is what a fantastic day it will be when Her Majesty, Queen Elizabeth the Queen Mother, gets her telegram from her daughter in the year 2000. What a party we'll all have! And I hope it gives Her Majesty as much pleasure as it did to my mother when she received two telegrams, not only the official one from the Monarch but also one from Queen Mum.

GEORDIE MENZIES

Shepherd, who taught me much. Top dog handler and crook maker

Geordie Menzies was the best 'kenner' of sheep I've known. At my farm of Gaskbeg at Laggan Bridge in Inverness-shire I had 500 ewes, and when they were all gathered into the fank he could tell you something about every one, which bit of the hill it grazed on, what sort of lamb it had last year etc., etc. It was a great gift which he used to the full and from which he was not distracted by T.V., as he lived his life for his flock, they were meat and drink to him (although he did enjoy drink of another kind on occasion as I'll divulge later). He had lots of other gifts too: he was a first-class sheep-dog handler and one of the best horn stick makers I have known. But as usual I go too fast – let's start at the beginning.

Geordie was one of a namely family of shepherds, the Menzies of Urlar, Aberfeldy. He used to tell the tale of how they were given their boots at the November 'term' (the 28th) and they were taken away from them at the May term (28th) and it was just too tough if there was a snow storm in early November or early June, and I've seen both in my time. Those were the days when children were given clothes for Christmas presents, so the boots, although a 'present', were only allowed to be used for six months!

Like many another from the land George volunteered for the Black Watch in the '14 to '18 war and he had to falsify his age to join up. Having had a whiff of gas, which was to bother him for the rest of his days, he was lucky to return to his beloved calling (and what higher is there in the land?) What a devastating effect the First World War had on this country. Not only did it decimate whole rural areas, but I believe it lost us our Empire, as the Colonial Officers, diplomats etc. for the post-war years were slaughtered – and slaughter is the only word one can use for what passed for fighting in the trenches.

I first met Geordie when he was head shepherd at Arrivain just over the border of Perthshire in Argyll. The farm was the furthest west of those owned by Ben Challum Ltd. over which I had been appointed as manager. The farm at the

Geordie Menzies

Geordie Menzies, on the right of the photo, who taught me so much about sheep, and with him John Russell, who opted out of the B.B.C. to become my cattleman and was one of the 'terrible trio' I had to deal with at the Granton Show in my Presidential year. They are grooming 'Kinloch of Fordie' who went on to be the Reserve Champion at Oban in 1954 and sold at the top price of 360 guineas (today's top price: 20,000 guineas!)

time carried two thousand Blackfaced ewes, but is now owned by the Forestry Commission, who over the years have bought up all too much land that hasn't grown good timber. The farm in question is a prime example, as a very small proportion is growing timber whereas the rest is planted with what Nicky Fairbairn so aptly described as 'lavatory brushes'.

Geordie had his brother and sister plus another shepherd to help him run the place – changed days indeed when now, with feeding, in-wintering, modern dips and medicines, four-wheeled motor bikes etc. he'd be lucky if he got anyone else to help him at the busy times of the year! What a superb dog handler he was, and I always remember his tears, for he had a soft side to his nature, when his good bitch fell over the cliffs on the 'Ben Dhu' hirsel. It was the late forties, and long before the days of 'All Creatures Great and Small' and 'One Man and His Dog'. Veterinary science had not progressed as it has since, and the dog, which hadn't been too well, obviously had 'hard pad' which was just being diagnosed about then. How those sheep dogs did the colossal mileage they did in those days I'll never know, as their only food was maize soaked in hot water or oatmeal porridge, and the only protein they got all year was at lambing time when they found the odd placenta (lamb bed). But one thing I do know, the dogs then could shift an old ewe stamping at them from behind a boulder and also shift a bulk of sheep, whereas the modern Border Collie has been bred for trial work on golf courses or similar flat areas. Strange how we Scots, famous throughout the world as stocksmen, can muck up some of our native breeds. Some master breeders called it refining the breed, but now most Border Collies can't shift a large number of sheep as they have no force. All too many Clydesdales have their hocks so close together and their feet are so big they can hardly pull a cart; the Aberdeen-Angus bulls have been bred so small they can't bull a cow; the beauty of the Ayrshire cow's udder has become so important that some stocksmen forgot about the milk it was meant to produce, and I could go on, but as usual I digress.

Sadly Geordie's brother's shepherding ability was not up to Geordie's, and Duncan Stewart my boss told me to dispense with his services. Geordie, who had quite a quick temper, said that if his brother was to go he too would leave.

It just happened at that time (1951) that Duncan Stewart thought his son was coming home to run the Estate, and this also coincided with me being offered the tenancy of Gaskbeg. As I had to dispense with the whole family, I 'fee'd' Geordie for Gaskbeg. He and I had many happy years together and seldom disagreed, with one notable exception, and that was about funerals. This was because, although he never went to church, he attended every funeral in the district wearing his famous bowler hat, which was green with age! In those days there was no way a shepherd could afford a dram, so they naturally took every opportunity of occasions which included free drink such as funerals and weddings (though Geordie always maintained there was more drink at a funeral than a wedding!)

Drams were also available, and often free, at communal events like sheep dippings and shearings, local agricultural shows, ram sales etc. I remember one February (the worst month for funerals) my three men – yes, these were the palmy days of lots of labour – were away at five different funerals leaving me to feed all the stock. I'd had enough by the last one, and as it was for Donald Tolmie from the neighbouring farm of Blargie whom Geordie couldn't stand, I said, 'Enough is enough, you did nothing but fight with him when he lived'. Back came the reply, 'Ah, but you must forgive them when they die.' 'Nuff said.

Then there were the sheep sales, which are the culmination of a sheep farmer and his shepherds' work. It is always a very long day and one full of tension. In my early days at Gaskbeg I had an ancient but trusty ex-army lorry, on top of which was precariously perched a sheep float, with a home-made upper deck that could be taken out to make the float into a cattle truck. There were no new fangled ideas like ramps up which the lambs could run onto the deck – we just threw them up.

We'd had a particularly good sale and Geordie as usual had 'drawn' the lambs well, i.e. had them like 'peas out of a pod' and not a wrong one in the lot, something all too often missing at lamb sales today. Geordie decided to take home a present to his wife, and this was a marriage that had had its turbulent periods. As she had always pestered him for a posh dinner set he invested in that very thing in a well known china shop in Perth, one of the few that still remains forty years on. We had a dog in the cab of the lorry, and Geordie was terrified it might break his precious china, so he put it (the china) in the bag containing the sawdust that we always carried to cover the sheep deck, and placed it safely in the forward corner of the top deck. As was our wont in those far off days before the breathalyser, fast cars and articulated lorries, we stopped at a few well known hostelries. Our last at Dalwhinnie then had as its 'mine host' Duggie Matheson, one of nature's gentlemen, and one who was more than kind to those who lived from the land be they farmers, shepherds, stalkers, keepers, etc. So it was natural that after a sheep sale those of us from the Badenoch District stayed there for quite a bit. Suffice to say that on the day in question Geordie and I returned to Gaskbeg in, shall we say, 'goodish fettle'. Burns in 'Tam O' Shanter' talks of Tam's wife 'gathering her brows like gathering storm', and I suspect that our wives were in the same mood. But Geordie was determined to put things right with his magnificent (and for him expensive) dinner service, so with great difficulty (and against my slightly more sober advice) he clambered onto the top deck. On his way back he forgot there was no ramp, fell arsie-tarsie from at least four feet, shattered every piece of china, stumbled shakily to his feet and said, 'I think I'll buy her fish next time, Captain.'

If you think I'm only writing about Geordie as a character because of the times he 'had the drink taken' you'd be wrong. I could go on about the long, long hours he put in for me and the perfection of his work that was his hallmark, but it's boring stuff to write about. Lambing time was non-stop for Geordie, as we lambed on the hill then whereas now they either have their ewes inside or at the least 'inbye' i.e. off the open hill. In Geordie's day we thought we would soften the ewes if they were fed too much or were brought in, and as a result all too often ewes lambed with all too little or no milk to feed their lambs, which meant a fantastic amount of work for a shepherd. Then there were the long days in the summer when we 'neighboured' with five other farms, gathering the sheep off the hills to mark the lambs and clip the hoggs (the young replacement ewes without lambs). These days meant starting off before 5 a.m. and finishing anytime at night from 7 p.m. to 10 p.m., and then off to another farm the next day. Then there was the hay making, a catchy business in northern climes, before the ewe clipping neighbourings began and the whole sheep stock of the Laggan Bridge area, I could only guess well in excess of 12,000, had to be gathered and shorn. Geordie was much in demand because not only had he the best dogs in the district but he was a top-class clipper. Showing sheep has always been one of Geordie's hobbies and he used to tell how he spent hours and hours plaiting the long wool that was fashionable in the Blackface sheep breed in his young days. By the time he came to me I was buying them as short a fleece as possible, as I'd found out at Ben Challum that the resultant ewes were much better milkers.

But, long or short wooled, Geordie was an artist at 'bringing out' sheep for show or sale. He was largely responsible for resuscitating the classes for Blackfaces at the Grantown-on-Spey Show. The show just after the war was mainly supported by the cattle breeders of lower Speyside, but when I joined the committee in 1952 Geordie made sure that I had the Blackface sheep classes reinstated. The 1955 show I will never forget as (a) I was chairman (b) I had an extra good cross calf that was bought after it was second in its class, and went on to be overall champion at the Scottish National Fatstock Club and at Smithfield, and (c) my three men all got paralytic! Not only was I chairman but I did the afternoon commentary, during which I was summoned to the marquee where the Young Farmers were preparing for their act, and my young tractorman, an especial favourite of the family and normally a teetotaler, had tried to still his nerves by 'partaking of the cratur' with disastrous results! So I asked a neighbouring farmer to take him home at the end of the show and put him up for the night so my family would be none the wiser. I rushed back to the 'mike' and just had time to see and congratulate Geordie on winning the sheep championship. I asked him would he be sure to get someone to help him load the sheep in the lorry, as I would be last to leave the show. The Chief of Police always had to be entertained after his men had seen the last of the cars out of the park (and thank goodness there weren't the number forty years ago that there are now). After I had said farewell to the Chief I saw my cattleman (who had left a good job in the B.B.C. to come to learn about farming) who had the good heifer calf in his charge. I told him not to let the neighbour, in whose lorry he and the calf were travelling, have too many stops on the way home because the calf, although five months old, was already starting to bellow as it needed a suck of its mother's milk. John, the cattleman, who was devoted to the calf, assured me they would be home before I was.

With a feeling of tremendous achievement after a good show, having done more than my share of the work, which is the chairman's duty, and doubtful privilege, I set off to the sheep lines where I could see my lorry was the only one remaining. My thoughts were centred on a dram or two, a hot bath, a good supper and bed. Imagine my shock when I opened the door of the lorry to put in my coat and crook to find Geordie snoring his head off with a beatific smile on his face. Well, old boy, wherever you are now, although I swore at you then, you had done me proud that day with the number of tickets you had won for me and you are completely forgiven. Although anyone reading this who has loaded sheep on his or her own without a loading bank, and up a steep ramp, will understand why I cursed Geordie, as he hadn't even been bothered to load the sheep before he got fu'.

So it was home without even someone to chat to about the high points of the day, one of the nicest things about showing (especially to castigate the judge if one hasn't won much!) After I had got the sheep (and Geordie) sorted out and back to Gaskbeg, and as I was enjoying my first dram, the phone rang saying it was Raigmore Hospital and to tell John that his wife had given birth to a daughter, their first, and could she speak to him? I said he would be home any minute and I'd get him to phone. My drams did nothing for me as the hours ticked past six o'clock, seven, eight and nine, and eventually at half past nine the lorry lights weaved their way between the trees that line the Gaskbeg drive. Out jumped, or should I say stumbled, John who was about to regale me with all the wonderful hospitality they'd had on the way home and how much 'Highland Princess', the heifer, had been admired by one and all. She, incidentally, was bellowing her lungs out in the back of the lorry! It's the first time I've ever thrown a bucket of water over anyone, and then I said, 'Now phone Raigmore Hospital, your wife's had a baby girl'. All John said was, 'I hope she's as good looking as "Highland Princess".' That was the day that was!!!

Geordie's winter nights were spent fashioning the most lovely shepherds' crooks: the horn from Blackface rams, in the years before they fed them so hard which now makes the horn soft, and the shanks from hazel. Nowadays he would make a bomb selling them, but then, when wages were peanuts, he used to take literally an armful to the Perth 'cast ewe' sale, which was the great meeting place of all the Blackface worthies, and he'd give them away.

In summer he spent hours and hours, as he had the patience of Job, training a young dog which he would eventually sell for what would now be regarded as a pittance.

I always remember when T.V. first came in there was a public showing in the Laggan Hall of the first set to be seen in our district. It was a well known personality being shown, a Bing Crosby or a Frank Sinatra. Donald, my youngest son, was coming away from the Hall and asked Geordie, 'What did you think of that?' to which the reply was, 'Just a big star in a wee picture!' Words which some of you may have seen on your screens, as Donald now has a share in, and directs, a T.V. company called just that.

Sadly T.V., which has done so much for us, has lost us all too many of the Geordies of this world, who used to make so much of their own entertainment. Apart from his stick-making and dog training Geordie was a regular and good Scottish dancer, and like so many of his generation who had had to entertain themselves he was a first-class raconteur. I loved the story he told of how he and the shepherds from Lochtayside had to walk the ewe hoggs through the hills to the railway siding at Dalnaspidal (bits of which can be seen to this day). The hoggs were being sent to the lower Speyside farms, to grow on sheep clean pastures, be away from the rams and ease the pressure on their home hirsels. The shepherds had to allow extra time in case of inclement weather and wanted to meet up with their pals to get all the news. In those days of steam there was an extra engine put on the front of the train at Blair Atholl to pull the train up to Dalnaspidal called the 'Pilot'. The Pilot's driver was given money by the shepherds to bring them a bottle (or two), but on one occasion the driver decided it would be wasted on the shepherds, with the result that there was more than a little confusion when the special sheep train arrived!

Because of technology the modern shepherds, for whom I have the highest regard, don't spend the hours and days that the Geordies did in the old times, just looking at their flocks. I started writing up this character by saying he was the best 'kenner' of sheep I have known, and although a lot of that would come naturally to him because of the way he was bred, a lot more came from those hours and hours simply studying sheep and their ways and habits. Good stocksmen willing to ignore the old adage 'what is this world so full of care, there is no time to stand and stare' are getting few and far between.

I was proud to work with Geordie, who tried to curb my impatience and made me lean over many a dyke and just stare, and there was always something to see – ewes moving because of that fox we saw slipping throught the rocks, that impending storm to judge by the cloud formation and the shift of the wind, that tup, easily seen because of the amount of red keel (paint) on his back, that was nowhere near where he should be among his ewes, etc., etc.

Because of your tuition, Geordie, I was once stalking some years later with two keen-eyed hill men many years younger than myself, and I saw a fox long before they did when we were spying at a herd of deer. Thanks, Geordie, for your tuition and your forbearance.

I have more than a little admiration for modern shepherds but because of modern technology they haven't had to learn the hard way as had the Geordies of this world and it bred 'characters.'

LORD MACKIE OF BENSHIE, C.B.E., D.S.O., D.F.C., LLD.

Peer of the Realm, a great Liberal and a great friend.

Of all my characters George must be the biggest not only in stature and, at times, in girth, but in the way he does everything. When he comes into a room he dominates it with his presence and usually with his voice as well. There's a saying in Aberdeenshire that the Mackies are like whales, 'they only come up to blaw'! But, my goodness, they have a whole lot to 'blow' about. From very hard beginnings, the Mackies now farm large acreages north and south of the Border. Of course they aren't everyone's cup of tea, as 'you're no doing any good 'til they're a' agin you', as my old friend Jim Wilson used to say. The Mackies have done more than well, not only on good farms, and not always by farming conventionally, but they farmed to make money. They have prospered in public life as well, Sir Maitland, Lord Lieutenant of Aberdeenshire, having been a brilliant chairman of numerous boards. Lord John became a Labour peer, and had Hugh Gaitskell or Nye Bevan become Prime Minister would undoubtedly have been Minister of Agriculture to a Labour Government.

Then there was Jean, of whom all too little is heard, who was brilliant in her own way but was slightly overshadowed by her husband, J.R. Allan. He wrote so well about the land and I enjoyed broadcasting with him. They bred a character called Charlie – writer, broadcaster and musician – of whom more will be heard in Scotland as the years go on.

But George, the youngest of the family, is the one whom I was to get to know best, partly because of our interest in farming and partly because of our mutual belief in Liberal policies and some form of devolution for Scotland. For all his row of decorations George had a hard start in life: like the author he didn't do too well at College, so when his father's grieve (foreman) packed in, George got the job, aged seventeen. This, I might say, was unheard of then, and I can just

Lord Mackie of Benshie

Lord Mackie of Benshie, friend and confidant, seen among his favourite tatties 'Golden Wonders', which he and the author agree are 'abin them a''

imagine the boys ganging up to make a fool of the boss's son. He had four and a half horsemen (i.e. one man to each pair of horse and a 'loon' – laddie – to the spare one), two cattlemen and an orraman – a 'Johnnie a' thing' who had to do anything including the garden.

So George decided he would prove himself from the word go. As it was the spring of the year they had to empty the cattle courts which were full of dung. The horsemen would come in with their two carts and each horseman would fill one and George the other, which he made a point of having filled before the horseman filled his. He proved his worth and won the day, but as he admits, 'I was buggered, Ben'. I'll bet he was, as he was filling four carts to each horseman's one! His wages were fifty pounds per annum, but being the boss's son he also got five percent of the profits.

He tells the tale of how one of his father's best employees made up his mind to leave. These were the pre-war days when the farmer went to the worker and asked quite bluntly, 'Are you staying or leaving?' This would be in March, because the terms when workers moved were either May 28th or November 28th, and if asked in March the worker had time to get his garden dug and ready for sowing. When Maitland Mackie, senior, asked this very good employee if he was 'staying or leaving' and was certain the answer would be the former, he was dumbfounded to hear the man say the one word, 'leavin'. Old Maitland, who didn't want to lose the man, said, 'Is there something wrong with the house?' 'Na, there's naething wrang with the hoose.' 'I pay you over the odds, you know.' 'I ken that maister, you've been unca' guid to me.' 'Are your horses not good enough?' 'I've the best pair in Aberdeenshire.' At which point old Maitland said, 'Well, why in all the world are you leaving me?' Back came the reply: 'It's like this, Mister Mackie, I'm getting to like the place and that means the fairmer has a hand on ye.' There speaks the independent Scot, an independence that has so much good about it in certain circumstances but so much harm in others, and from what George says this would be one. Even when I came back after the war to manage farms and estates the movement of farm labour was frightening. I well remember seeing a family leaving what was then a very modern cottage to go to what I knew to be a damp, rat-infested one, because the husband wanted to be near the 'boozer'. The wife was a sweet lass who helped in the farmhouse, but she and her children were chucked up on top of a few bits of furniture all in one tractor bogey, to start a new life and start the kids at a new school. The wife and children were all crying, and who can blame them, I often wonder what sort of impact all those moves had on the children.

As the farm profit was about the seven hundred pound mark, George's share was thirty five pounds, which modern readers will laugh at but, oh boy! to those of us young and single in the late thirties, with thirty five pounds in your pocket the world was your oyster! My trusty old 500 c.c. Rudge motorbike cost me five pounds, and lasted two years until I left it in a ditch when I got my call to arms.

However, George, as he has done all his life, aspired to greater things, and like many a Scot in the thirties decided to try his luck south of the Border. Major Keith, from Aberdeenshire, a name revered in farming to this day and of course a friend of George's father, said he could find a job for our character on his Weasingham farms in Norfolk.

The Major told George he was sorry he couldn't give him the foreman's job as he already had a first class man. However the Major offered him the stock manager's job (pardon me, George, if I laugh up my sleeve, as I have the highest regard for you but not as a stocksman!) and at the enhanced pay of five pounds per week. He was stationed near Swaffham in Norfolk and was in charge of five dairy herds of Ayrshires, two flocks of sheep and two herds of pigs. He was to find out early on in his job why Scotsmen were in such demand in East Anglia in the thirties. Quite simply because with our hard climate and often poorer soil we learned to work harder than they had to in the South to make a living, also our markets were further away and until the advent of modern transport we didn't get as much for our produce. These factors meant that the farm labour in the south was much more lackadaisical than in Scotland, where the same difference occurs between, say, Easter Ross and Argyll, it's a matter of climatic conditions. Well anyway, George's first job was to get the head dairymen out of their beds in the morning, and by chopping and changing his rota he put the fear of God up them. I can just imagine his great bulk appearing in a doorway and the cattleman wondering if the bull had got loose!!

But these years had a great effect on George's future farming operations, as like Major Keith he was always willing to try something new. He always recounts how farming sugar beet revolutionised Norfolk, which, with its light sandy soil, didn't until the introduction of beet have a really suitable cash crop.

Cocksfoot grass with its tremendous root growth was another thing that Major Keith used, as the sandy soil of Norfolk can blow all too easily. George still talks about the bell tents that the shepherds used at lambing time, but when I was lambing Southdown ewes in Sussex I had the luxury of a caravan. Nowadays most ewes, except on the largest hill farms, are lambed in sheds. But one thing remains constant now as then, that lambing shepherds find there is nothing like a drop or two of whisky to revive an ailing lamb and a drop or two more works wonders for the lambing shepherd!

Third September, 1939, was a day to be remembered by G.M., as that's when he joined the R.A.F. He'd always had a hankering for the Airforce and had been offered a short service commission in 1937 but didn't take it up. I think George would be the first to admit he is one of the lucky survivors, as only about one thousand out of the many thousands survived three tours of duty in bombers.

His description of his early operations should, like all George's stories, be told by himself, but he managed to bomb barges in Le Touquet instead of Boulogne and they aren't exactly near each other! In the spring of forty-one he was sent off to the Middle East to cover Malta and Egypt, with ops to the Western Desert, although those of us in the army thought that the R.A.F. had forsaken us and every plane was German! He did an instructing job after that, but managed to get away to be part of three big raids of one thousand bombers over Germany. After this he was appointed Observer Captain of Aircraft of 149 Squadron, but managed to fall out with the C.O. It's not difficult for one to fall out with George, who can be very set in his ways. But 1944 was a great year for him as he married Lindsay, who was a good wife to him for forty two years until she tragically died of cancer.

I always remember Lindsay, because she was a very family person and when George bought Brae Roy near Roybridge in Inverness-shire she was adamant that I should take my boys up there for picnics, as we were not too far away at Lagganbridge. She was a first-class mother to their three daughters, but Jacqui, whom George married in 1988, seemed to fit in with his love of travel more than did Lindsay. But of course both George and Jacqui had been married before, and their families are grown up, so they not only knew each other but knew what they were taking on.

George had the great distinction of being awarded the D.S.O. as Flight Lieutenant in February 1943, and the D.F.C. in June, having done eleven operations over Berlin during that period.

It was after his demob that I got to know him. We were both back after active service, his more active than mine as I spent all too much of the war in hospital. There was quite a gap between those of us in farming who gave up the chance of being in a 'reserved occupation', and went off regardless, and those who stayed at home and in many cases made a lot of money. I know of a case where one farmer who was in the Territorials went off to fight and came back to find his tenanted farm had been given to another farmer who already had another two farms!

Not only the ex-service side but so many other things we had in common brought us together. We started up a small advisory service, and looking back now we should have gone on with it judging by the number of land agents who are springing up like mushrooms, I remember we did a job for someone well known in Royal circles, where our conclusion was that the manager was well and truly on the fiddle. However we were told they didn't want our advice. Dougie/Geordie/Jock or whatever his name was, was 'indispensible': so were the profits of their Estate to his taste for whisky!!

As I said earlier the Mackies weren't always conventional farmers but they looked on farming as a business, whereas so many of us, myself included, looked on it more as a way of life. George was in everything that he thought would make a profit, dairy bred cattle for example, that were bought cheap to fatten for so-called beef that I wouldn't be seen dead with on any farm of mine. Nor would he eat any of the resultant meat, as he is a great 'gourmet', and although he always laughed at me for keeping cross Angus cattle he always told his butcher to sell him nothing else!

I may sound a bit disparaging about George's farming methods, but if this is so I have absolutely no reason to be, as he has made more money out of it than I ever did. But when it comes down to basics we had completely different outlooks. I am horribly traditional, which nowadays is rather looked down upon; for instance, when I saw someone ploughing snow into the ground the other day I cried out in alarm, but my youthful farming companion saw nothing wrong in it. All my farming days I was what would be called a conventional farmer and always let a neighbour test out the 'new fangled' ideas before I took them up. George, on the other hand, like all the Mackie family, was an innovator, and without innovators where would we all be? Just look at his strawberries, which I think were a great financial success, his Golden Wonder potatoes, which he rightly started growing when everyone was beginning to get fed up with the tasteless rubbish that is being sold as tatties today, or his nephew Mike's ice cream, or the many other things the Mackies have done for Scottish agriculture (and themselves) that the Coutts' traditionalism has failed to do.

Probably it was his out-wintered pigs that brought George and I more closely together. He had got the idea from Richard Roadmight, who had done tremendously well with them in the South. He had a farm on light soil on the Hampshire Downs, and realised that a section of the British buying public was getting fed up hearing about sows being kept in stalls and piglets being reared in artificial conditions. The clincher of course was that his 'free range' porkers made more than others. George, never slow to jump on a wagon, started up the same system.

Where he went wrong was that it was at the time he bought Braeroy, a middling hill farm in Inverness-shire at the head of Glen Roy, and he decided to put his pigs up there. Well, the rainfall up there is anything up to eighty inches in the year, and the ground is not light and porous as it is in Hampshire. For generations people up there had found that Blackfaced sheep and deer were what paid best, and because of that and my experience in these fields, George got me in to advise him.

I always remember the first day I went up with him, and said the first thing we do is get the head shepherd and go round the marches (the estate boundaries) so that we can see what the land's like. It took us all day. I was fit in these days – George less so, as he was farming arable land while I was gathering sheep regularly in the Lagganbridge area. Anyway when we got back to the Lodge George produced a rather special bottle of malt whisky and said to the head shepherd, who of course had shown us round, 'Well, Neil, you'll have a dram after that long walk, and thanks', to which Neil replied, 'Well, the wife will have the tea ready but if you insist!' It wasn't long before the first drams were down the hatch and George said, 'You'll have another, Neil?' Back came the same reply, 'Well, the wife will have the tea ready but if you insist!' By the time it came to the third round, and as George has a lovely heavy hand when it comes to pouring a dram, the bottle was getting low. George said, 'Sorry, Neil, this will need to be the last'. To which Neil replied, 'Mr Mackie, it's a good thing I wasn't born a woman, I can never say No'.

I had some happy years with George in Braeroy, but those west coast hill farms are not the easiest to be made viable unless one is living on them and running them oneself, and as he had political aspirations, which he pulled off, he decided to sell it. To his dying day (as he rightly thinks he has taste) he will regret not realising that he had a valuable painting hanging on his stairs, which could have given him a good profit on the estate.

During George's stay in the glen his brother John, now the Labour Peer and then an M.P., wanted to bring a busload of agricultural engineers up to the local crofting township half way up the Glen because he reckoned that the crofters had the right ideas about sharing everything. (He should hear some of the fights, both verbal and physical, that I've seen and heard at crofters meetings.) Anyway the great day arrived and the bus disembarked its cargo of engineers. John asked the representative of the crofters to explain how the system worked, to which the answer was something like this: 'Well, you see, we put the tups out in November, we lamb the ewes in April, we clip the ewes in July, we dip the ewes in August, we spean and sell the lambs in September, sell the cast ewes in October, buy a tup or two then and share the profits'. End of discourse, which was meant to be a great lecture on how socialism worked in the Highlands!

I know I will be unpopular for saying it, and I have many crofter friends, but like small farmers they are sadly an anachronism who are now dependent on outside employment to keep their crofts going. The snag is we all want a higher standard of living, and many of us want the way of life that the crofters enjoy, but 'you canna' dae baith'.

As you'll read in the chapter on Robbie McHardy, I was thrilled when George was elected M.P. for Caithness and Sutherland in 1964. No-one had worked harder for a seat than he had, and anyone who used to travel the road to Wick before the new bridges will know just what ghastly journeys he had to make from Angus. I was sad when he was dumped in 1966, but much of the cause must have been that he spent so much time in Edinburgh sorting out things at Headquarters. As a life long Liberal supporter I'm always sad that so many who back the cause are so 'airy fairy', and I can see my old pal going through the Headquarters like a dose of salts!

So who better to be made a peer in 1974, while still young enough to use his brain and common sense in the Upper House. When he was elevated to the peerage he took the name 'Benshie', which those living locally know is the pronunciation of 'Ballinshoe', George's farm from 1945 to 1990.

Since those Braeroy days our meetings have been social. 'Benshie' pheasant shoots were notable for the lunch and the fact that the host was an even worse shot than the author! As to the lunches, if you want to see someone who can really carve, and it will always be the tastiest ham, beef, you name it, I can recommend My Lord. Also if you want the best wines served 'ad lib' I recommend My Lord's table, no longer now at Benshie, but at Cortachy and just as generous.

When George married Jacqui in 1988 I had the great honour of being asked to make the speech at a typical super Mackie feast in the Kirriemuir Town Hall. It's extraordinary how when one thinks of Kirriemuir one either thinks of J.M. Barrie or the famous 'Ba' of Kirriemuir', but I now connect it with my old pal George.

When I wrote to him for some wartime dates for the period before I knew him, he itemised them, e.g. Demob, 1st January 1946. Elected M.P. 1964. Etc., etc., with many more in between, and he finished with 'Hopefully died 2010'! Dear George, good men are scarce and you are one of the few characters of whom I have written who is still alive, so please stay around to await the Monarch's telegram.

BILL KERON

Neighbour and friend, and other horsemen

Horse ploughmen are a dying breed. It's strange how one sits down to write about characters, thinks about the few famous ones one has known, has a dram with a local and suddenly realises what makes a character. Bill Keron, whom I am proud to call a friend, and I have much in common: a love of life and the countryside, and of horses, a dram and the old ways of farming which we have enjoyed.

'Grass Sickness' is a disease that has afflicted horses in Scotland since I was a laddie, looking after Highland ponies in Perthshire in the late 20's and 30's, and before. I remember well when, after I failed my veterinary exams so brilliantly in 1936, I went as a groom to one of the top thoroughbred studs in England and told my fellow grooms about 'grass sickness'. They laughed me to scorn, and in reply I said 'wait until it hits one of the top studs in Newmarket and we'll see some real money put up for research'. For once in my life I've been right, and I'm sorry they didn't open a book on my prediction as I'm useless at making money! But now there is real money going into a research programme because Newmarket has been smitten by all too many cases of this 'Will o' the Wisp' disease. Rumour has it that the great 'Mill Reef' died of the dreaded disease, but its symptoms, which I have seen all too often, are so like a really bad colic that anyone who hadn't the experience of Grass Sickness might think it a severe case of colic.

Where in all the world does your character Bill Keron come into this diatribe, Ben? You have every right to ask. Simply that he and his generation in Strathearn, in the years between the wars, had to keep a spare pair of Clydesdale horses because there was every possibility that one or two of their working horses might succumb to the dread disease. And of course because of their losses and their love of the breed, they nearly all kept a Clydesdale mare whose progeny they hoped would not succumb to the disease, and would go on to be

Bill Keron

One of the last oat stacks to be built in Scotland, for the T.V. serial 'Strathblair'.
Bill Keron, who kept the stacker right, e.g., 'too much out on this side and a bit
more hearting needed etc. etc.' is second from the right in the photo, with 'Corriebeg'
in the background

broken and become one of the 'Pair' on the farm. Breaking a horse nowadays for riding, jumping, eventing etc. is a very slow careful process of lungeing, long reining etc., but Bill reckons that in those times they needed their horses broken quickly and they 'yoked' (harnessed) them as soon as they could. The golden rule with a young horse, who wouldn't be too fit, was never to let him stop of his own accord at the end of the drill, because ever after he would always expect to do that (and get a bite of grass); but to let him stop half way up and then turn him at the top. What pearls of wisdom those old horsemen have to give the new generation who sit in their heated tractor cabs listening to some modern so-called music, meantime harrowing or rolling in a peewit's nest, because they are listening and not looking. So speaks an 'oldie' who loved his pair of horses as did Bill.

Perth was the Mecca of working horses for Central Scotland just before, during and after the war, and Bill and I were agreeing lately that sadly work-horse sales were not devoid of what is now internationally known as 'Horse Trading'. The number of horses we saw that went through the horse ring in the MacDonald Frazer's Mart, Caledonian Road, were Legion (for they were 'many' as the Bible says!) But you would see the same horse(s) come back through the ring week after week, having failed the vet. As Bill and I agreed, horse dealing is not the only form of trading that is not as honest as it might be, because as I write in 1993 some people have had their fingers badly burnt dealing with a famous insurance firm! Bill and I share, as I have said, a love of showing our stock. I know it's a disease and, as we say in Scotland when a disease can be transmitted 'it's smittal', then it must be smittal, as my dear wife Sal is as show daft now as I used to be. Bill and I agree that, not being as young as we once were, we are leaving it to other members of the family to do the work. But we are not in such a bad way (or as old?) as one pal, who when I asked him why he was no longer showing answered 'all my judges are deid'.

Horses that have cold shoulders, i.e. are chary of putting all their weight into the collar, can be a pest. I remember well when I was learning my trade as a shepherd in the thirties, and as the last-joined recruit one was expected to do everything, we were bringing in the hay coles. These are small hay stacks about six to eight feet high that were brought to the big hay stack in the farmyard by a horse 'slipe'. The farm on which I was working at the time has a nasty 'snib', a small hill of about forty degrees, going up into the farmyard. The mare I was working was 'cold shouldered', got half way up the brae and came to an abrupt halt. The time was 12.15, fifteen minutes after we should have 'loused' (broken off for dinner). An irate head shepherd came to demand what the hell was holding me up as it was past 'lousing time'. He, knowing the mare, sized up the situation in a oner and said, 'I'll shift the bitch'. He went into his cottage, grabbed a hot potato out of the pot, came back, plonked it on the mare's rear-end, shall we say, whereupon the mare clamped her tail onto it, which made the potato not only firmly fixed to her tender parts but also turned on the heat. She shot up the hill and I had one helluva job stopping her, in fact she went three times round the stackyard before a very shaken and ashen-faced boy climbed down off the hay bogey. In my time with her that mare never stopped on that hill again.

Bill to this day shows Clydesdales, which like the Shires, Suffolk Punches and Percherons are gentle giants. He says that his father and he never had much trouble breaking them, which they did at three years old. About a month before they were due to be broken the horse would be stabled, having been halter broken as a foal and handled off and on from then. During that month they would be bridled and would be introduced to their collar and the rest of their harness. One of the main reasons for this was to get them onto 'hard' feed e.g. oats, hay etc., as on grass alone they would be too soft to work. Their first lesson would be long reining, which they did with an old horse alongside to which the three-year-old was attached in case the youngster decided he wanted to set off into the blue horizon! Then they attached a log behind the young horse, but drove the pair with the old horse pulling nothing, and so it progressed, with the plough being the first real implement the young horse had to cope with. A two hour stint was as much as one would expect a young horse to do for a start, as one only needs to see an old picture of a pair of horses in a plough to see how much effort they have to put into the job.

I asked Bill what was the hardest job he did in the horse days, and he said spreading quick lime – when one had to shovel the 'hot' lime out of a cart with a shovel – but I think he was thinking more of the hardest job for himself, not the horses! I think pulling the old binders must have been one of the hardest jobs for the horses, as we always needed three to pull them and I was always sorry for the one on the side next to the crop because they were usually muzzled. This was so that they couldn't eat the crop, for the reasons that (a) if they ate green or half ripe oats all day they'd land up with colic, and (b) one member of a three-horse team holding back can completely spoil the rhythm.

Thinking of Bill's worst job with a horse I have no doubts about mine. When I took Gaskbeg at Laggan in Inverness-shire in 1951, I was strapped for cash to put it mildly. The farm was needing lime and potash very badly. The lime was spread by an old rotating wheel fixed onto the differential from an old car, and when shovelled out of a bogey drawn by my ancient (and cheap) Ferguson tractor was hurled 'o'er a' the airts'. If a bit too much was deposited no harm was done, as the deficiency of pH in the soil required tons per acre to put it right. Sadly with potash it was only necessary to put on hundredweights per acre to adjust the balance. I decided to buy an ancient horse-drawn fertilizer spreader, which would make a fortune at a farm sale today, and a cheap Highland pony to pull it. 'You gets what you pays for', and I spent more time running after that manure spreader than I did walking! Potash in those days came as basic slag from

Belgium in jute bags, and after handling it one looked blacker than a chimney sweep! I understand that one was inhaling steel particles from it, but the authorities weren't so worried about the odd death then as they are now. However after charging round fifty acres behind that horse I was ready to go to the cemetery.

Bill and I were discussing how interesting it is that stock are often connected with characters, and in our time one of the 'greats' was Pete Sharp, who exported hundreds of Clydesdales to Canada and America. Some Scots in 1993 might say too many, as we are short of good stallions, but the truth of that I wouldn't know. My first meeting with Pete was back in the forties when my then boss, Sir James Roberts Strathallan, was on the War Agricultural Executive Committee and asked me to drive him to check up on something at Bardrill, Blackford, then farmed by Pete's father, Messer Sharp. Sir James knew Pete had been sent to the public school, Strathallan, and when he enquired from Messer how he had done, back came the reply, 'there he is under that dung spreader, it's a' he's fit for, as he only came back with his school tie to show he'd been there but no exam results'. How wrong Pete's father was, as he became a great ambassador for Scotland when he went out to America to sell Clydesdales.

I well remember when I was out at the famous Toronto Winter Fair, long after Pete had made his mark with the Canadians, and he asked me up to his Hotel room for a dram. As is usual on these occasions, nature calls – as my old Dad used to say, 'What's the difference between the lavatory and the cemetery?' The answer is nothing – 'When you got to go you've got to go!' Anyway, when I got to the loo I looked in the bath which was literally a foot deep in empty bottles! When I got back to Pete I said, 'obviously you don't bath when you're here', and he replied, 'Good God no, there's no time to bath. I only come over with one spare shirt and one spare pair of socks and buy new ones when the others are dirty!' When I think of all the useless clothes that I've never worn but carted around the world I think Pete was more than a bit astute.

But back to Bill. When I was asked to be the Agricultural Adviser to the T.V. serial, 'Strathblair', which was set in 1950 to 1951, and I had to reproduce farming scenes of that era, Bill was an obvious choice as someone to help me out. I had to help the Director to screen the handling of Highland ponies, grubbing turnips, gathering the hay with an old fashioned 'Tumblin' Tam', carting potatoes and then, after the first series during which, in the script, the Highland pony was burnt (but not, readers, in reality) the progression to a Ferguson Tractor with a binder behind it and with actors and actresses having to 'stook' the oats and then stack them. Who better than Bill to show them how it was done? But more about 'Strathblair' when I write about another Scots character I knew well.

Bill, like so many of us who like good stock, goes to Orkney for his holidays. There is a warmth about the Orcadians that is becoming a rare thing in this country of ours, where greed has taken over from need. Not only are the Orcadians warm and friendly, but because of their long winter nights and terrible gales plus excessive charges for transport, they have to make the most of their land, which means producing quality products. In my humble opinion they are the last bastion of quality beef producers in the whole of Britain, although I think in the next year or two many beef-producing farmers will realise that it is only quality that will be wanted.

Orkney produces one of the top malt whiskies in 'Highland Park', and also brews a beer called 'Home Brew' that could blow your head off! So when I was being driven around one of the islands on one occasion and we were following a car that was weaving from one side of the road to the other, I said to my driver, 'that chap's stocious drunk'. He replied, 'Na, na, that's old X.Y.Z., he's got cattle on both sides of the road'. When I drive South on the motorways I realise that old X.Y.Z. has got the right idea and the right priorities!

Having judged at many Agricultural Shows for the last forty years I realise just how essential good stewarding is, i.e. bringing out the stock all together, be it cattle, horses or sheep, so one doesn't see too much of the good or bad points of one animal while awaiting the arrival of the rest. Also it's important to have read the Show schedule and to know which animals are eligible for which special classes, rosettes, championships etc. Bill Keron is one of a dying breed of good stewards, as more and more young farmers only drive tractors (usually with Radio 1 at full bore) and don't handle or know about stock. When they come to steward a show, because father did it before them, they are lost. I always remember stewarding for the great stocksman Bob Adam. (Plenty of people thought he used his great ability to his own advantage, but as he started with nothing who could blame him?) Anyway as I was saying I was stewarding for him and he had just made me pull into line a class of very middling yearling heifers. I couldn't see an obvious leader and stupidly I asked Bob (who had said, 'Give out the tickets, Ben') 'Which end do I start?' He replied, 'Any bloody end!'

Sadly the Bill Kerons of this world will get fewer. Radio and T.V. have been good to me in this last half century but they prepare everything for us, whereas in the old days when Bill drove his pair of horse he had time to think about things and didn't have to have decisions made for him. The age of the horse, which he and I loved, made the countryside the way most people love it. The mechanical age is already destroying and will destroy it.

SIR WALTER COUTTS, G.C.M.G., M.B.E.

The last Governor and only Governor General of Uganda and a dearly loved brother.

I feel it only right to include 'Wally' as he was later called, although as a boy he was always known as Fleming, because of all our family he was the one of whom father and mother would have been most proud. I always laugh to myself nowadays at the thought that the first three in our family were given Fleming as one of their christian names. Mother's father, Sir John Fleming, was one of two Dundonian brothers who started life selling papers in Dundee, but both went on to make good in different ways. My grandfather founded a very successful timber business in Aberdeen which is going particularly well now, thanks to the oil boom. As well as making a success in business he became the Lord Provost of the City of Aberdeen and also their Liberal M.P. However because mother married an impecunious minister she was given a house at St Fillans in Perthshire and that was her lot.

Judging by his autobiography the old man was a fearful snob (those who start with nothing nearly always are the worst) and as Dad, who had no use for money, used to say, 'Money is a great divider'.

Sir John's brother Robert went to London and founded the world famous Fleming's Bank, and I had the pleasure of managing the estate of Blackmount he bought in 1923. I had twenty-five happy years managing the estate for Robert's son, Major Phil, and latterly for his grandson, Robin. Thanks to his generosity I am penning this book in my own cottage, so if grandfather didn't do the Coutts family any favours his relations have.

Getting to know mother as I did in her latter years (and she didn't die until she was five days short of being one hundred and one!) I found out she was vastly

Sir Walter Coutts

Sir Walter Coutts G.C.M.G., M.B.E., Governor of Uganda from 1961 to 1963 and the only Governor General until its Independence, much loved and respected brother

proud of her father's success, and secretly hoped some of us might be asked to join his timber firm or at least be left a bit of cash, but she was wasting her time on both counts. So Fleming became Wally, or as my family called him, 'Uncle Wol'.

He it was who got to St Andrews University and then on to St John's, Cambridge, which father would have dearly loved myself and brother Frank to do, but we made our way to the top of our professions by different means. When Wally came back from St. Andrews he was always dead tired and used to laze about the house, and I remember Dad saying to him, 'Don't come home and bestow your tediousness on us'. Dad had a lovely full vocabulary.

When Wally was at St Andrews he became the President of the Student's Union and as such was responsible for looking after the Rector of the University. In his year it was none other than General Jan Smuts, who fought brilliantly for the Boers against us in the Boer War, but in the Second World War was to become a personal friend of Winston Churchill's. He was instrumental in getting South Africa involved on our side, though there were many South Africans with German leanings. I had an interesting follow up to Wol's contact with General Smuts, as when I was on an International Wool Scholarship in South Africa in 1964 I stayed with a Mr Brocksma who had been Jan Smuts' lawyer. He had retired and bought himself a vineyard near Stellenbosch and was enjoying every second of his retirement, starting every day with half a bottle of sherry for breakfast!

I don't know if it's the sea air of St Andrews, but when my daughter, Rosalie, went to the University all those fifty-six years later, she came home just like her 'Uncle Wol', bad tempered and tired, and 'bestowed her tediousness on us'! But that University made a great job of my brother and my daughter, and if I have any regret in life it is that I didn't have the honour to be one of its students.

During his time at Cambridge Wol played one game of rugger for Melrose at the Greenyards, and I was also in the team. Those were the days when there was only a handful of spectators in the stand, but Dad, although himself a hockey player, was always present. There was an outburst of swearing from the scrum when it was right in front of the stand, whereupon a broad Border voice on the touchline said, 'There go the meenester's sons!' That was the same year that Charlie Drummond was starting his great rugby career and his old father, the St Boswells saddler, used to stand on the touchline and no matter where the ball came out of the scrum used to bellow, 'Gie the ba' tae Cherlie!'. Perhaps he was right!

When Wally left Cambridge in 1936 he had set his mind on the Colonial Service. The Sudan was reckoned to be the tops then, so he put in for it, only to be turned down because of a 'dicky ticker' which was to plague him for fifty-two years.

I can't help feeling that as usual someone above knew better, as he was to do a much better job in Kenya and Uganda than he would ever have been able to do in what was then called Anglo-Egyptian Sudan. Luckily he was the Coutts with an ear for languages and was known in Kenya as 'Swahili Coutts', which language was to stand him in good stead when in 1961 he, as Chief Secretary, was preparing the country for multi-racial government. A good friend of the family said Wally was willing to sit all day among a circle of African Chiefs, and after they'd all had their say, would quietly wag his index finger at them (a habit he continued to use to us all to his dying day), tell them what was to be done and break up the meeting. They all went away thoroughly pleased because they'd all had their say. The white settlers weren't too pleased with Wol's appreciation of the black Kenyans' point of view and demanded his resignation, but when one looks at the bloodshed in South Africa and many other African countries seeking independence it is no wonder the late Sir Martin Gilliatt, Secretary to the Queen Mother, said to me, 'Your brother did an outstanding job for Kenya in its fight for independence.'

I must say, having gone there a couple of years ago, it seems a lot more stable than most of the other African countries that have got their independence. After the white settlers got their way and he was recalled to London for what the Colonial Office called 'a long rest' brother Wol was appointed Governor of Uganda.

He loved his home leaves as he was a passionate Scot, and would have dearly loved to have retired there, but he and his super wife, Jinty (always known as 'Bones' for obvious reasons, as all the years I've known her she has never carried an ounce of flesh), could not stand our Scottish winter climate.

He used to love to come to stay with me on whichever farm I happened to be, and though he was hopelessly unpractical, used to take a mower, tractor, you name it to pieces, called himself 'the bloody marvellous mechanic' and the machine never worked properly again! As for stock, he hadn't a clue and would always be in the wrong place when one was moving sheep or cattle. But everyone to their own job. I, with my impatience, and lack of an ear for languages, could never have attempted the Colonial Service as a career. Funny how one's ear can take some things and not others. Dad, who had a beautiful speaking and singing voice, passed on some of each to most of us, but Wol, who used to love singing 'The wee cock sparra' at the Caledonian dinner in Nyeri, had a poor singing voice but an ear for languages.

His elevation to Governor of Uganda couldn't have come at a more difficult time, as there was a violent election going on and 'the lost counties' in Buganda were heaving, with jungle drums throbbing, as the Buganda tribe fought the Banjoro. However Uganda got its independence in 1962, and Milton Obote, their first Prime Minister, asked that Wol be the Governor General. Our youngest brother, Philip, had chosen the Colonial Service as his vocation after wartime service in the Royal Air Force, and was posted to Uganda: it was a bit embarrassing for him when his big brother was appointed Governor in 1961. So much so that he turned down promotion that year, as he was sure his fellow District Commisioners would think it was a 'fix'.

I was having problems at home, so when Wol invited me to visit him at Government House, Kampala, I jumped at the chance and thank goodness I did, as the colonies are disintegrating and there can't be many Government Houses left. Everything was so beautifully organised, one was served by people who wanted to serve you but were not servile, and there was a peace and tranquillity, which seemed to emanate from Wally and Jinty, about the whole building. I always remember the 'Piri-Piri' sauce that was produced on Sunday lunches, and was so hot it was called 'Piri-Piri Ho-Ho' because it caught your breath so much you had to let it go with a 'ho-ho'.

When we went driving in the Governor's car Wol would make the driver stop whenever he saw a collection of villagers, and he'd get out and talk to them and their faces would light up. No wonder he was popular – most 'Brits' wouldn't even stop, never mind know how to speak to them. Then there was the famous safari when Obote asked Wol to go north to an area graced by the lovely name of 'Opottipot' to see if it couldn't be turned into a Safari Park with airstrip, hotel, apartments etc. as Kenya was doing. Actually it would have been ideal, but Amin and his lot took over shortly afterwards, and Uganda, 'the Rose of Africa', is only just coming together again after thirty years of bloodshed.

Wally, Philip and I boarded a light aircraft at Entebbe to fly to 'Opottipot' and as we were all over six feet and all fourteen stone the pilot was rather worried about whether he could get the aircraft off the ground. He told us, luckily after we had landed, that he just made it and no more! It was to me a never to be forgotten Safari. Not only did we have the First Battalion Uganda Rifles to look after the Governor General, but we had the top game warden in Uganda to find the different species for us, and to top it all each night our camp was set up for us with everything one could want. If you haven't sat under an African sky, sipping a cold whisky, having had a shower or bath to wash off the 'stoor' and then eaten some grilled venison of the dozens of different species of deer, and heard lions roaring in the not too far distance, then you haven't lived! But I knew then as I know even more now I was a lucky, lucky laddie, and no way did I take the experience for granted but thanked God for it. It did however completely spoil me for the other two safaris I was to do in 1964 and 1992: they just weren't in the same street.

In 1969, when Wally was appointed Vice-chancellor of Warwick University, I doubt if he realised how useful his handling of warring tribal chiefs would be! He was famous in Kenya for getting up on a table, in Fort Hall in 1948, and telling a warring tribe, who were hell bent on killing the chief and himself, to get to hell out of it, in Kikuyu of course; which they did. He was to do the same thing at Warwick University in 1969, when rebellious students had spent all day railing against the hierarchy. He gave them all day to argue, then got on a table and told them to go home — and they went. That's leadership of the highest order.

After that period at Warwick University came some years that sadly, at his time of life, were something in hindsight he could have done without. Fleming's Bank, founded by mother's uncle, asked him to take on the chairmanship of Pergamon Press at a time when the infamous Captain Robert Maxwell was fighting to regain control of the business. I, at that time, was managing the Flemings' Highland Estate, and used to get all too many phone calls from Richard Fleming, the then chairman but not my boss (that was his uncle, Major Phil), telling me to get my brother Wally to see sense and back Maxwell. I don't know the exact words I used in reply, but they were roughly, 'If Wally says he's a twister, then a twister he is'. Wally, Richard and 'Captain Bob' are all dead now, but my goodness the Coutts family have nothing but scorn for the last named.

Wol's health deteriorated during his two years at Pergamon Press. His ticker, never good, showed signs of strain then, but with his ingrained sense of loyalty he felt he had to see the job through. Brother, Brigadier Frank, was in charge of the V.I.P.s at the Commonwealth Games in Edinburgh that were supposed to be sponsored by Maxwell (but I believe he never coughed up the money) and in Holyrood Frank had to take the 'gallant'(?) Captain aside and tell him that the party was the Monarch's, not Maxwell's, and that one doesn't put one's arm around the Queen's shoulders even if a certain jumped-up Aussie thinks you do! And as for me, well, I didn't realise that Aberdeen University Press who were good enough to publish my *Bothy to Big Ben* were owned by Pergamon Press, and when he did away with himself or slipped overboard or whatever they owed me four hundred-odd smackers! So you see the great Bob Maxwell is not a pin-up of the Coutts family, although another Maxwell in this book was!

Thank goodness there were some more interesting and less exacting jobs for Wally to do before he and Jinty decided finally to retire to Australia, to be within hailing distance of their son and daughter and their grandchildren, and also to be in the sunshine which they found indispensible to them after all those years spent in its rays!

He particularly enjoyed his secretaryship of the Dulverton Trust, and I was strangely to come against him during his period in that job. I had done an advisory job for Lord Dulverton back in the fifties, when he had been talked into putting a mass of hill cows onto a barren estate, Eileanrigh, by the dreaded Mam Ratigan Pass, over which all feeding had to be carted. He realised something wasn't right and called me in. The place could have carried ten cows at a pinch but not one hundred! I remember well that at the time I was doing the job I was asked to judge the local show, of which Lord Dulverton was President, so would I like to stay the night before with him and Lady Dulverton at their shooting lodge? Little did I realise they were about to divorce and were not on speaking terms. I will never forget sitting, after our evening meal, with a fire smoking as only West Coast Shooting Lodge fires can and damp streaming down the walls, Lord Dulverton with a pile of 'Passing Cloud' cigarettes on one side of the mantlepiece and Lady Dulverton with a pile of 'Three Castle' cigarettes on the other (or it may have been vice versa, but does it matter?) They never spoke to each other except through me, all most embarrassing. But by the time Wol was Secretary of the Dulverton Trust, Tony Dulverton had remarried Rosy which obviously was a great success as he was a changed character.

Sadly, like all too many people who come from the south to own large estates, Tony, basically a kind man, wanted to oust a tenant who was farming his land well because Tony thought he could do it better, I, at that time, was doing the odd valuation and arbitration, and was called in by a firm of estate agents to give my professional advice. I was highly embarrassed to find that my big brother was present at the meeting of landlord, tenant and their agents. The tenant won his case: and I have never been more 'chuffed' in my life than when I was going into the Lochaber Showground near Fort William a year ago (where I was due to judge the Highland Pony Working Class), and the tenant (both of us now thirty plus years older) came up to me, almost wrung my hand off and said, 'You're a chentleman, Captain Ben. I thought you were bound to side with Lord Dulverton since your brother Sir Walter was his right-hand man. The wife and I are still there and very happy, just thanks'.

It may have taken thirty plus years to say, and probably a dram or two, but oh! how it warmed this old man's heart. It's sad that doing the honest thing isn't often rewarded these days even with a 'thank you', which doesn't cost much.

It's very hard as a brother to be absolutely fair when writing about one's kith and kin, but one thing I know I can say is that his terrific sense of loyalty, honesty and always being kind to those who were on the bottom rung of the ladder came from Father, Mother and our manse upbringing. He was a great supporter of the Church, and although Chief Secretary, i.e. second in command, in Kenya, and well able to delegate the duty, he was always at the door of St Andrew's Kirk in Nairobi on a Sunday to welcome personally everyone with a cheery word. As his brother I always think his greatest assets were his sense of humour and his humbleness.

For all his great achievements, and they were great – as how many could say they were instrumental in helping a country like Kenya to independence? – it was his humility that I admired and how he could laugh at himself. Father always said there was nothing like a manse upbringing as 'you never had any money and you met all sorts, had to get on with them, understand their problems and like them, whether you wanted to or not.'

Wol, you certainly did just that and are greatly missed by the Coutts family, who are mighty proud of you.

DONALD LAMONT

Agricultural entrepreneur, excellent shot and judge of ponies

When I went, as tenant of Gaskbeg Farm, to Lagganbridge in Upper Speyside in 1951, I had to start making a new set of friends from those in Strathearn where I had been domiciled from 1943 to 1951.

One person I did know, however, through my interest in Highland ponies, was Donald, who lived over the hill in Blair Atholl. Donald was the first agricultural entrepreneur I knew. He began in the hard up thirties, and young farmers in the late eighties and early nineties who moan about hard times should count themselves lucky compared with those of us who were farm workers then, as I was, or those who farmed. But Donald, who was a tenant on the Duke of Atholl's estate, realised that the only way to make money was to take one's crop and/or stock right through to the purchaser, or as near as possible. So what did he do? He rented the Duke's inbye 'parks' (now famous for holding the big three day event horse trials), and there he grew the top seed potatoes and feeding rape (not the yellow stuff so commonly seen today). Blair Atholl is 800 feet above sea level, so the dreaded aphid which carries so many potato diseases doesn't like the area much, and as the parkland hadn't been ploughed the land was wonderfully clean. But where Donald scored was that he went south himself to Lincolnshire and the other English counties that use Scottish seed to grow the ware (the eating potatoes) for London. Donald was a striking figure of a man, always immaculately turned out, and although he never married many a lassie's gaze turned his way. So although I didn't know him in the thirties I can just imagine him visiting the wealthy farmers in Lincolnshire and the wives telling their husbands that they had to buy Donald's seed potatoes!

The oil from the rape he grew is ideal for finishing hill lambs AND the rabbits won't eat it! He used to buy top grade Blackfaced wether lambs, which could be got for nothing in the thirties, put them on the rape, then he would book railway wagons and take them to Smithfield Market in London. Again he went down himself to sell them. He was a man before his time when you think nowadays all farmers are being exhorted to produce what the customer requires – there's nothing new in this world.

No wonder when I got to know Donald really well in the fifties he was able to turn out so immaculately and his manners were also so perfect: he knew everyone. I well remember when I was showing a Highland bull at the Royal Show in Windsor, in the days of the travelling shows, it would be 1955? The cattle, as usual in those far off days, were lined up in the middle of the ring and the pageant, whatever the theme, was paraded round the outside. That year, most appropriately for Windsor, it depicted Royal connections with Agriculture. Imagine my surprise when Donald passed leading a Highland pony which was harnessed to a light horse vehicle. Donald was dressed up as John Brown and the very old lady in the vehicle was Queen Victoria. As they passed I said to Donald, who was dearly loved by the ladies, 'couldn't you have done better than that?' indicating the old lady. To which he replied, 'come round to tent 216 after the parade, Ben'. Yes, we were all in tents in those far off days before permanent show grounds; and how much more fun it was sleeping in the straw beside one's stock. When I got round to 216, there was Donald, false beard etc. all removed, and as I came in he turned and said, 'Ben Coutts, can I introduce you to Queen Victoria, alias Anna Neagle'. What a man, what a character. Anna Neagle, the famous actress of her time, was born a Robertson and her clan belongs to Struan just across from Invervack.

Yes, 'Don Q', as he was known, was before his time. He got his name of 'Don Q' through his exploits as a first-class gun shot who represented Scotland in the International Clay Pigeon Championships. Before the last war many of the top Clay Pigeon shots were keepers on large Scottish estates, and as they were taking time off their work (although in these days they got no official holidays) and because they were probably using their bosses' cartridges, they all used pseudonyms – though why Donald used one beats me, as he was his own boss and very much a law unto himself. One of the great shots of that era was Angus Cameron from Glenkinglass on the Blackmount Estate, whom I was proud to stalk with when I was factor there. He called himself the 'Silver Doctor' – I always meant to ask him why. His great feats in clay pigeon shooting I have recounted in *Bothy to Big Ben*, so I won't bore you with them here.

Donald was more than useful to me (and himself, I might add) when I took on the factorship of Gaick and Glentromie in the fifties. The new owners were extremely kind bosses, but few of the 'young entry' had ever shot a grouse. Although the 'do-gooders' hate the thought of grouse being shot, they don't realise that if grouse stocks are left to multiply, which was happening in the fifties, and they aren't shot, disease and worms can wipe out a stock in no time. We had a grand hatching year in the early fifties (does it matter which one?) and

Donald Lamont

'Don Q', alias Donald Lamont of Blair Atholl, farming entrepreneur, Highland pony breeder, first class shot, seen here in centre of front row as captain of Scotland's Clay Pigeon team, with on his left Ewan Ormiston, another great Scottish character

I asked Donald and his great pal Ewan Ormiston to come to help out so that a reasonable 'bag' would be shot to keep the breeding stock right.

Ewan Ormiston could, of course, have a chapter to himself in this book as he certainly was a character. He it was who pioneered pony trekking in the Highlands, although many others have claimed that accolade. Ewan was responsible for culling red deer in the Highlands during the war, and it always annoyed me that because the stalkers he used were such good and rapid shots, non-resident landlords said he was using machine guns to mow them down, something he, who knew about and respected deer, would never dream of doing. He once gave me one of the outstanding stalks of my life, high above the upper Spey, on the Cluny Estate, on a bare flat top. He said, 'we're going to turn our backs on those hinds' (who are always flighty) 'so they don't see our faces, and get into that peat bog one hundred yards ahead'. I just couldn't believe it but it worked.

Donald and Ewan had much in common, they were firstly and essentially Highland gentlemen that could mix in any company. They both were good at their jobs, Donald with his farming and Ewan with his hotel business, his letting of sporting estates plus a butcher's business selling excellent venison. Long before the Germans, Italians etc. were all coming to Scotland for sport Ewan was arranging for Americans to come over, and one of the results was that he used to send grouse shot on the twelfth of August to the '21' Restaurant in New York. Probably many Scots not resident in Badenoch or Atholl would know about them as two regular members of the Scottish International Clay Pigeon team.

Just after the war both of them used to take grouse moors and re-let them, keeping one 'butt' for themselves. They must turn in their graves when they see the price that has to be paid to rent a grouse moor today.

When I farmed Gaskbeg I drove an ancient but trusty old Austin lorry so that I was able to transport my own stock to market, this normally being Perth. As it was, thank goodness, before the days of the breathalyser, the Atholl Arms, Blair Atholl, was an essential stop before tackling the dreaded Drumochter Pass. I know the breathalyser was necessary, but my, how it has ruined the social life of the Highlands. Our cars and lorries were so sturdily made and so slow in the fifties that I can't remember a single person in my area being hurt, far less killed then, but oh dear, how things have changed. As one stopped for a 'refresh' at the Atholl Arms one always either found Donald already ensconced there, or one rang him up to tell him to come over for a dram. It was at one of those many meetings that he rekindled my interest in Highland ponies, and told me that although he hadn't got a good mare for sale, Ewan Ormiston had. From that mare and Donald's famous Glengarry III, I bred a superb colt foal that was castrated, by mistake, not by my authority. Yes, Donald and Ewan had the love and knowledge of Highland ponies in common, and were excellent judges of the breed. Among many subjects we discussed at those meetings I remember well telling him that I had seen the great 'Glenbruar', one of the really potent sires in the Highland pony Breed. Glenbruar had been bred on a farm just opposite Donald's, but never had a chance to be bred to good mares until he went to Donald McKelvie's stud at Lamlash, Arran. In the twenties the Coutts family, if they were lucky, were invited to stay with father's session clerk who was a lawyer in Glasgow but had a holiday home in Arran. His name was Hugh Buchanan and I think was Donald McKelvie's lawyer. Certainly he knew him well, and so I got the entrée to see the stud and lead some of Donald McKelvie's ponies at the Highland, and what a thrill that was for a horse-daft laddie. Glenbruar was the stud horse then, and getting on in years, but what an advert for the breed he was. The year he was put down, 1931, aged 26, he had three colt foals born, all to be kept as stud horses – what a horse! I saw him in 1929 and am probably the only remaining judge of the Highland Pony Society who ever saw this great wee horse.

Then of course Donald Lamont and I would discuss local farming problems and new technology, on which neither of us was very keen! One night 'Don Q' asked, 'Have you been up Glen Fender, Ben?' When I replied in the negative, he said, 'Come on, I'll show you some super crofting land', and so, in a way, the television series 'Strathblair' was born. Forty years later I was approached by the then B.B.C. Controller for Scotland, Pat Chalmers, to find a site for a drama series about an ex-wartime Sergeant Major coming back to a Highland farm, and asked, would I be Agricultural Adviser? Toumagruie, which became 'Corriebeg' in the series, I knew to be vacant, as my son Hamish had been renting it and I knew he was not going back. Innes Smith, the farming tenant, was more than willing for us to use it, and like all the farmers in the area was most co-operative – what better way of diversification? But sadly some of those in the village of Blair Atholl were not of the same mind and killed the goose that laid the golden egg.

Although I had done quite a bit of T.V. for farming programmes I had never been involved with a programme of this sort which involves so many people. When we were shooting there could be thirty of us on call in one day, and although I feel the B.B.C. are right in making financial cuts, and there were many that could have been made in Strathblair, it would be sad if saving halfpennies is going to take over from artistic expertise.

The original team who planned the programme were Pat, the B.B.C. Controller for Scotland; Norman McAndlish, Assistant Head of Drama, who was to produce the first series of ten episodes but sadly left us after one or two episodes (I say sadly because he understood the countryside); Bill Craig, who did such a marvellous job putting Lewis Grassic Gibbon's trilogy on the box and who knows, understands and loves the land; and yours truly. I had not only to find the location but as I had come back from the war and gone to a farm like Corriebeg in 1951, I knew about the problems the 'Ritchies' would face. Bill

Craig was terrific from a farming angle, and kept phoning me up to find out what would be happening on a hill farm at certain times of the year, and also what names were used for certain implements, clothing, etc., etc. Sadly some of the writers after him hadn't even the decency to phone me up, and some of the gaffes were horrendous. I can't think why the Producer, Director and the Technical Adviser didn't all meet before every episode. Oh! I know I'll be told the Producer, Director and the lighting man would meet, but I would have saved the show thousands of pounds had I known what the Director was going to shoot. An excellent example of this was the Strathblair Agricultural Show, where the designers, who were marvellous, with my help set up a really first class Country Show as we had it in the fifties. However, of this we saw practically nothing but Highland dancers, who are not part of an Agricultural Show, tug-of-war teams wearing rubber soled boots which we didn't have in the fifties, and a Highland Pony Class. This had been organised by me especially so that Jennie's pony could be rightly beaten, but as we saw only one other pony the scene was a farce. The wonderful W.R.I. tent, the basket tent, the stalkers and ghillies in their estate tweeds etc., etc. were never even shown; what a shame and what a waste of money. I think if the Lord is kind and gives me another life I want to come back as a 'props' buyer, as they seem to be able to buy anything they think is right for a given scene without finding out whether a local might have the correct article or whether it is correct for the period.

But for all that I am full of admiration for the long hours the team worked. Breakfast would be outside on a cold hillside at 8 a.m., and they were lucky if they 'wrapped up' by 6 p.m. having had two short tea breaks and an hour's break for lunch (though I must say the caterer we had was first-class).

However it wasn't serious all the time, as I remember in the first episode of all on a terribly cold day with snow on Ben-y-Gloe. We were working in John Cameron's old fank, beside that super stone wall that divides the heathery hill and the improved 'inbye' land. We were dipping the hill ewes as we used to do in the fifties, to get rid of the keds, lice etc. before they lambed, so that the 'wee beasties' didn't get onto the lambs. I asked John for his own sake to provide yeld (empty) ewes, but there were one or two in-lamb ewes in the bunch he provided and one had started to lamb coming up the passage leading to the dipper and was put in one of the side 'buchts' (sections). When the camera is about to turn the Production Manager, a lady in this case, is the person in charge and usually says 'Quiet', then 'Action' when the camera turns and the actors start speaking. On this occasion when 'Quiet' was announced the old ewe was lambing and was grunting loudly. 'Quiet!' came the command for the second time but once again there were loud grunts. 'QUIET!' came the stentorian voice once more, to which one of my super team of shepherd/helpers (and I'll never know which) said, 'If what she's doing was happening to you, you'd be grunting too, lassie.'

Then there was the other occasion when we were filming at Corriebeg and the hens and cockerel were an integral part of a scene. The cockerel decided that one of his lady friends needed attention and as is the wont of cockerels jumped on and in two seconds flat was off. As one of my shepherds remarked, the cocks say 'wham, wham, thank you Ma'am'! When she saw this one of our well-known actresses was heard to exclaim, 'If that's all that happens no wonder the hens at Corriebeg look so miserable!'

Judging by the letters and phone calls I've had, many, many people enjoy nostalgia and country matters, and after all none of us need go far back in our parenthood to find forebears who were on the land. It's sad, to my mind, that Directors (although I have a son who is one) have far too much say and put what they call art ahead of what people really want to see. They also claim that they are governed by the 'ratings' which say the public want sex and crime! I would have thought you could have that just about twenty-four hours a day on any programme, whereas 'Strathblair' had scenery and nostalgia seldom seen on T.V.

Donald, you may think I've deserted you on this long digression, but I haven't because you helped make the programme what it was and you would have been a 'wow' as an extra on 'Strathblair'. You were always one who could judge a good filly and there were some super girls in the team! Thanks for introducing me to Glen Fender, and I'm only sorry you weren't still with us in 1991 and 1992.

LORD BANNERMAN OF KILDONAN

Great rugby player, Gaelic enthusiast and patriot

Although I went to Glasgow Academy and the great 'Baanie', as Johnnie was known, had been to our hated rivals, Glasgow High, he was a legend to me even then back in the twenties. And why shouldn't he be? The fact that he'd been capped for Scotland at rugger thirty-seven times and their captain on sixteen occasions would make any rugby-daft laddie put this man on a pedestal, no matter which school he attended.

Little did I think all those sixty years ago that I was to get to know my boyhood hero so intimately thirty years on.

Johnnie was a devoted Celt, and no wonder, as his forbears came from Sutherland and Uist. His great-grandfather, wounded at Waterloo, came back to Kildonan in Sutherland to find the family had been evicted, so he went to Glasgow where he married a Uist girl. When widowed, Johnnie's great-grandmother returned to Uist, but eventually her family had to return to Glasgow because of the potato famine and drought (I'll bet the islanders of Uist could do with one of the latter in the 1990's, but this was 1873). Anyhow, John's father, like so many Highlanders, prospered there and became a Senior Superintendent in the G.P.O. Also like many Highlanders of that era, he retained the Gaelic and also composed songs. The well known 'Uist Tramping Song' was one of his, and how Johnnie loved to sing it at the different social occasions on which we met.

The great man showed early prowess in sport at both his schools, Shawlands Academy and Glasgow High School. At the former he played a nifty game of soccer, and this was where he learnt to dribble a ball. From this skill came the days when the Scottish rugby forwards, led by Johnnie, rejoiced to the cries of 'feet, Scotland, feet' and put terror into the opposition, and how some of us

Lord Bannerman

The Great 'Baanie', Lord Bannerman of Kildonan, a great supporter of everything Scottish, dearly loved, greatly missed and badly wanted today

oldies would love to see that again! It would be in these formative years that he learnt not only how much he loved his native land, but its culture, its language and its religion. To his dying day, when all his friends attended the most poignant funeral service ever, at St Columba's Gaelic Church, he was a devoted believer.

After school he went to Glasgow University where he graduated M.A., B.Sc., in 1926. It was during that period that he met the great Donald McKelvie of Lamlash, Arran, who produced so many well known Scottish potatoes that tasted as tatties should. His best seller then was 'Arran Banner', and I wonder where Donald got that name from?

But my character was heading for greater things, and after Glasgow he got into a postgraduate course at Balliol, Oxford, where they were delighted to have him to play rugger for them and from where he of course got his 'Blue'. But that wasn't enough for the 'lad o' pairts', so he set off for Cornell University and travelled across America in an ancient Buick which Ray, his daughter, says devoured as much oil as petrol!

Back from the States and Johnnie was snapped up by the Duke of Montrose to look after his estates around Loch Lomond and also in Arran. He was also snapped up by a very good-looking farmer's daughter from Taradale, Sutherland, one Ray Mundell, and in the course of time they produced two boys and two girls. One of the latter was to become M.P. for Argyll, something that J.M. never achieved, but oh! how proud he would be of his daughter today. In a letter to me recently she said: 'He was my hero and my political inspiration as he was to so many others, not only in politics but in Gaelic, Rugby and his love of Scotland'. Ray, when you wrote that letter you little realised you were writing to the converted. I loved your father: he was the sort of man who, during the war, could turn a bemused platoon, a regiment, yes, even an army, into a fighting force, by pure personality and the gift of leadership.

The great J.M.B. spurned anything that smacked of professionalism in sport, especially in his favourite one, rugby. It seems ironic that on the very day when I'm penning this chapter Matthew Gloag's of 'Famous Grouse' fame have announced that they are putting one million pounds into a Trust Fund for international players which will give, I'm told, about £4,000 to each player towards their expenses. Changed days indeed, Johnnie, when you think that in your international days you, Jimmie Ireland (with those wonderful ten-to-two feet i.e. like clock hands set at ten to two that he used as hooker to scoop the ball in the scrum) and Luddie Stewart, all from Glasgow High School Former Pupils, used to come over by train from Glasgow on the day of the match! Not only that, you walked from Haymarket to Murrayfield! Changed days indeed, as now they have to get together for at least a week's training and everything is paid for including a dress kilt outfit if the team member hasn't got one, and a room for the night after the official dinner for the player and his partner, be it his wife, fiancée or girl friend! I don't think, like me, J.M. would approve of the latter, and certainly the members of St. Columba's Gaelic Church wouldn't. And remember how you only got one jersey (until it got ripped off you or it wore out) – well, now they get a new one every match!

Even long after you played, Johnnie, three players, Ralph Sampson, Donnie Innes and Ian Henderson, who had played in the Scottish XV in 1939, were recalled to play for their country in 1947 having all served in the forces, and were amazed to find that no blue jerseys with the famous white thistle had been supplied for them. When, in the dressing room just prior to the game, they asked Harry Simpson the secretary of the Scottish Rugby Union where their jerseys were, he replied: 'You got them in 1939'. End of story, and true at that as I got it from the late Ian Henderson.

Johnnie, like all great men you had faults, but yours were nice ones. Your idealism and fervour often took over from the practical. One of your fellow players told me that you called a team meeting on a train, which was then the form of transport, and after haranguing them for quite a bit you concluded, 'We've got to fix those Welsh forwards'. Voice from the back: 'Johnnie, we're playing Ireland'.

And in farming too you often let your idealism take over, and it was through farming and then from having the same political leanings that we met, followed by an association through broadcasting. Johnnie loved Scotland and especially the Highlands so much that all too often he got carried away with impossible schemes for rehabilitating crofters etc; and could one blame him – he was a 'voice in the land' and his great-grandfather had been evicted from his croft in Kildonan, Sutherland, all those years ago – but times had changed after the Second World War. I had been lucky enough to work with Sir James Denby Roberts Bart. of Strathallan Estate and Duncan Stewart of Millhills, and because of this Johnnie leaned on me heavily for agricultural input in the country areas of his Inverness-shire constituency. The former was an innovator in the sowing of seed potatoes and white crops in Strathearn and the latter was the best stocksman I've been fortunate to know, with whom for five years I was honoured to work. Sadly Duncan was so shy that many who could have benefited from his knowledge never heard his words of wisdom, but luckily for me (and probably unluckily for a whole host of listeners) he launched me on my public speaking and broadcasting career.

It was 1947, the year of the big snow storm, and Duncan had promised to speak to the Aberfeldy National Farmers Union, but when the day came he said to me, 'My duodenal ulcer is giving me hell, Ben, here's my speech, go and deliver it'. I can't say I delivered it verbatim, but my goodness how much common sense was in it, and how many young farmers today would be the better of hearing it. Things like, only breed the best stock, don't overborrow at the Bank, don't cross crop, look after your land, don't punish it etc., etc. All the sorts of things we of a past generation looked on as written on tablets of stone but which are now laughed at by the modern farmers.

When I was farming at Gaskbeg, Lagganbridge, in Upper Speyside in the fifties I was chairman of the local Liberal Association (a minute number of people then, when you think that in those days the local Laird sent out his car at elections to drive the old age pensioners to the polling station and the chauffeur said, 'Now you know where to put the X don't you?' And in the fifties you can guess to which party the Laird was affiliated!!) The local Liberal candidate was none other than John M. Bannerman, whom I got to know really well through our broadcasting on 'Farm Forum'. These were great days before everyone had a T.V. set, and village halls were full to overflowing. I remember once at Scourie that some of the young were sitting on the window ledges, the hall was so full. Johnnie was always a firm favourite, but as I've said his Highland idealism overlooked some of the more practical things that hill-farming required. However his character, his personality and his charm came over so well to the audience and over the air. His answers, to someone like me who was making his living from a hard hill farm 1,000 feet above sea level, were absolutely not practical, but he got away with it. It was the same at the political meetings, where I had to go ahead and start the meeting and try to hold the audience until the great man came, and he was always late. 'Sorry, Ben, but they wanted me to sing a wee song in the Gaelic'.

These were the days when even we Liberals could fill a village hall, and when he came in the whole atmosphere changed and one got a feeling of elation. George Mackie cites the time in 1964 when he, George, was standing for Caithness and Sutherland and Johnnie was to speak for him at Golspie. George had found the audience a bit sticky, but when word got round that John was due to arrive, there was a buzz of excitement, he just seemed to have the charisma that could charm an audience. During the period when J.M.B. was fighting Inverness we had a wonderful meeting in Beauly, where Alastair Duncan Miller, prospective Liberal candidate for West Perthshire, Maitland Mackie, prospective candidate for West Aberdeenshire and yours truly were supporting Johnnie. In the front row was the local laird, Lord Lovat, whom I knew through my association with the Beef Shorthorn breed. He got to his feet, and waving the Liberal manifesto in the air addressed me with the words, 'Ben, according to your manifesto you are going to do X.Y.Z.' I hurriedly turned to my friends on the platform saying, 'Help, I haven't read the manifesto'. To which they whispered in reply, 'Nor have we'. Such sadly was the organisation of the Party in those days, but happily this is the case no more. However that was only partly why Johnnie didn't win the seat in the fifties. It was mainly because we were more feudal then than we are now, and Johnnie would never spend enough time in Fort William. Like myself he loved the country folk and would have ceilidhs with them, but the votes were, and are still, in the towns as I found many many years later when I stood for Perth and Kinross. He was so magnanimous that he gave up Inverness-shire to go to fight Paisley where neither he nor anyone else in the Party – and my goodness we were thin on the ground then – scented a possible victory: but how nearly he pulled it off.

He very kindly said I could take his place as prospective Liberal candidate in Inverness-shire, but for personal reasons I couldn't accept and anyway, what a good M.P. they got in Russell Johnston.

Like all prospective candidates John had to tell a story or two to lighten up the more than dull business of saying what he would do if returned as M.P. (and I wonder how many politicians have kept those promises when elected?) My favourite, and I heard it often as I chaired many meetings for him, was to do with his policy of wanting more money put into Public Transport. This is forty years ago, and he was describing how badly served some of the islands were and how many hadn't even decent piers. One of these islands was being inspected by some Departmental officials to see if they should recommend a pier or not. At the same time as the officials were being returned to the MacBrayne steamer in an open dinghy, a Highland cow was being winched aboard as they used to do it in those days with a sling under her belly. And as Johnnie used to tell the story, 'She must have heard that the officials had turned down the island's request for a pier, because she showed her disgust as only a Highland cow can do, all over the officials and from a great height!' It always brought down the house, and the effect was partly because of his lovely voice.

No one who attended the 'great Scot's' funeral will ever forget it. That hardened old Liberal, Lord Byers, had hired a plane to take the then very few Liberal M.P.s to attend the service. The Gaelic choir absolutely demolished them, and Lord Byers, not known to be the most feeling type of man, was seen to drop more than one tear! Being a celt Hoosen just let go and wept unashamedly, and who with any real feelings wouldn't? Here we were saying goodbye to a great Scot, one of the greatest in my lifetime, and one we could do with today when so many small countries are wanting independence: but he was before his time.

If any reader of these slightly roughly put together portraits of people whom I think of as 'Great Scots' can remember a funeral where every policeman stopped the traffic to allow the cortege to pass, in this case from the centre of Glasgow to the cemetery at Drymen, I'd be glad to hear from them. But such was Johnnie's talent to be loved and respected by ordinary folk that the 'Polis' wanted to pay their last respects.

Johnnie, you were not the best chairman of a political meeting that I've encountered, but you had a wonderful gift of realising what the ordinary 'Jock' wanted, and you latched on to it.

How we in the Liberal Party in Scotland could do with you now (even if it was only to be 'Fear an Tighe' at those wonderful ceilidhs you ran for me all those forty years ago). But your honesty, loyalty (to party, religion, employer whatever) and sheer hard work for a cause (that cost you money, it didn't pay you money) is so lacking in politics today.

Your daughter Ray said you wanted an Assembly in Scotland 'because it was right'. Whether I see it or not is doubtful, but at least I'm certain it will come, as all minorities who realise that 'big' is not necessarily 'beautiful' want more say in their own affairs.

It was so sad that the great man never made the House of Commons, but typically when he was made a Life Peer in 1967 he was on his feet two hours later, making his maiden speech, something usually made weeks after being introduced. It was as one would expect a fighting speech, during which he launched into Gaelic, about having an Assembly in Edinburgh; and he said 'As soon as the equivalent house is set up in Edinburgh I shall gladly take the shorter journey'.

'Baanie', how badly we need your leadership, charisma and charm in Scotland today. You were never on time for a meeting, and had not the greatest of singing voices, which you always said only got you your gold medal at the Mod because there was a hail storm raging on the tin roof of the hall where you were being judged! But, my God, you had so many gifts and so much charm, and you had so many friends, that those left miss you badly.

You would have been proud to see your daughter, Ray, win Argyll in 1988 and hold it in 1992. So although you couldn't win it yourself you bred one that could. You would also have been proud to see your grandson, Shade Munro, wear the famous Scottish International Rugby jersey in 1993 and 1994. You yourself were a great Scot if ever there was one.

ROBBIE McHARDY

Shepherd, adviser and friend.

Of all my characters Robbie is by far the hardest to write up, mainly because we were so close for so many years but also because shepherding was his life and as such he didn't go out and do other things. He was brought up in Strathdon, just about as near the top of the country as you can get, son of a well known shepherding family. Although we were very close for some thirty-six years, he never divulged to me much about his family background, but he was such a gentleman, with the most perfect manners and with loads of commonsense and a good brain, plus the good looks of well bred folk and royalty, that it made me wonder whether somewhere along the family tree there had been an 'out cross' as we would say in the stock breeding world! After all, they say 'it's a wise man that knows who his father is'! Whatever Robbie's back pedigree might have had in it, there is no doubt his father was his father as I never saw two so alike and with the same attributes.

When George Menzies, of whom you have read, wanted work for his sons and I was already overstaffed at Gaskbeg, I made him and his elder son shepherds at Cluny Estate which I was managing, and advertised for a married shepherd for Gaskbeg. Among the many replies was a beautifully written one from Strathdon (only later was I to learn that Anne, Robbie's wife, did all the scribing as he looked on that as woman's work!) This letter very sensibly stated that if I wanted to know more about the applicant I should contact Donald Grant of Blacksboat, Craigellachie, at the Aberdeen-Angus Bull Sales. I say this letter was so sensible because, having employed labour for fifty years, I know only too well that a letter, plus references, can tell one all about the person's good points but nothing about their faults! Whereas when one can talk about the future employee with the former employer you can get the 'WOIKS' as the Americans say.

In this case Donald, after dispensing the most colossal dram of pure nectar out of his huge flask, said, 'Ben, if I had a job for Robbie you wouldn't get him', and you couldn't get a better reference than that! It transpired that Rob had worked for Donald before the former had married Anne, and she, like some other women I know, didn't like him being an employee, and as a result he took a croft on Sir John Forbes' Allargue Estate right next to the famous Cock Bridge. I say famous, because the first road to block with snow drifts every winter is the Cock Bridge to Tomintoul road. Rob's wife was English, and had come up to help in one of the many shooting-lodges in the area when she hooked Robbie, who was the first to admit to me that he was foot loose and fancy free until she nabbed him. Like many fit shepherds when he had finished his very hard day's and often week's work, he found solace in the liquid which has made Scotland famous throughout the world. Not only that, but Robbie in his single days, when working for Donald Grant, would be shepherding close to distilleries where they dispensed 'the real McKay', that lovely clear stuff which Robbie always called 'Mothers' Milk': in fact one of his toasts was 'If my mother had milk like this I would ne'er hae been speaned (weaned)'.

I know in all my characters I may have brought in references to 'the cratur', but it has given me enormous pleasure and naturally my characters have enjoyed it too. In Scotland with its wet and cold climate many of us, and I include myself, may have come to depend on the odd dram, but how often it has helped! Whether it be with a speech, a ceilidh or just reminiscences like these.

Anyway, Anne decided on life in the croft. With hindsight Rob told me this was a non-starter, as it wasn't big enough and was far too high-lying, with grass not coming until June and the first frosts coming by the middle of September. Luckily his Laird, Sir John Forbes, was able to employ him during the grouse-shooting season, as Allargue was, and still is, one of the ideal moors for grouse.

Thank goodness (because grouse will only eat heather) no one has been able to rear them artificially, as they do pheasants, and that, plus the fact of their coming down wind at 60 m.p.h. with their jinking flight, makes them the most sought after game in the world. Allargue is special because it consists of two saucer-shaped corries, and as grouse fly with the contours one can drive them around the bowl and then back again over the same butts, and then move the guns up and do the same again. Areas like Strathdon with their short summers and long winters certainly need the infusion of cash that the 'toffs' who shoot grouse bring in.

Apart from helping during the season of grouse shooting and deer stalking, Rob and Anne had to make the most of what the croft could produce. Luckily Anne had green fingers and as her father, a cantankerous old so-and-so, had been a head gardener, she grew more green vegetables in the Strath than anyone else. They were able to sell some, but the amount of cash they raised was a pittance to what they needed. There were of course some sheep, but not nearly enough because of the small acreage, and there was no common grazing that usually goes with a croft. The common grazing is a large expanse of hill land where the crofter could run his ewe stock, only using his arable land for finishing lambs, holding sheep for sale, keeping rams separate from ewes etc. Then of course they

Robbie McHardy

On the left, Robbie McHardy ready to set out with the author to 'gather', i.e., bring in, the 550 Blackfaced ewes on Gaskbeg, Lagganbridge. (Neither of us were top dog handlers but we always seemed to manage!)

had a house cow, an essential then. I might add that I had one until I was seventy, and everyone said what a waste of time and money, with which I totally disagree, as you got your milk – real milk from which you skimmed the cream that made porridge taste as it should – you made your own real butter, the skim milk fed the pigs which gave you real bacon, and any spare went to the hens that laid real eggs, not these insipid shells that pass as eggs today. Oh yes, there was a lot to say for the house cow. Then of course they kept poultry, and to my dying day I will never forget a story that Robbie told which epitomises how hard those times were. On this occasion they had twenty geese ready for Christmas, and all pre-sold on condition they were plucked and cleaned. The week before Christmas Robbie and Anne were both struck down with a terrible 'flu bug and neither could get out of bed. The doctor got the postman, himself a crofter as all were part-time, to milk, feed and water the cow. He also organised another neighbour to kill the geese and deliver them to Rob and Anne, who duly plucked them while feeling at death's door, in bed, and you want to see the down that geese produce!

Robbie always said that if they hadn't had the geese for sale there would have been no Christmas presents for their two sons nor a New Year bottle, which no one who called himself a Scot could be without! How that marriage survived after that I'll never know, but thank God it did, because not only did they have that terrible 'flu bug, but 1953 was one of the last really bad snowy winters we have seen. The McHardys said, 'enough is enough', and applied for my job at Gaskbeg.

So Robbie came to Gaskbeg and made a very 'duff' start. As he hadn't needed a dog in the latter years on the croft he had to buy one, and like me he had other gifts but not dog handling. Of course the first time he was running this new dog, which was a disaster, who should be passing but George Menzies, whom you will have read was a superb dog handler. 'Who's this you've got in my place, Captain, that can't even handle a dog?' he said. But time was to tell me what a super choice I had made. He was, as I've said, someone with a brain, and had he had further education he could have done anything as so many Highland lads did in the twenties and thirties. They became doctors, lawyers, went to colonies and dominions which we still ruled in those days, and they ran them with honesty and fairness. When I left school in 1953 the school notice-board was full of jobs vacant in India, Africa, Argentina (where I was sore tempted to go but I'd been such a bad student I hadn't the qualifications); and of course the top shipping companies in the world were in Scotland then and offered all sorts of interesting jobs to the qualified. But Robbie had made his mind up to be a carpenter (and what finer calling when one thinks of the most famous one of all, 2,000 years ago). However his father said the family needed some money coming into the household urgently, and remember I'm talking about the twenties and thirties when this country was in real recession, not what they call a recession nowadays in the nineties, when no one is as poor as the poor were sixty five to seventy years ago. Old Dad McHardy was dearly loved in the Strathdon area, and a most generous man with the pittance he received for his dedicated work.

Rob would have been a wonderful joiner as he was meticulous in all the wood-working jobs he did for me, and as I, like my father before me, can't hit a nail in straight, it was a joy to have Rob do all those wee jobs so essential to keep a farm and farmhouse looking right.

So, thank goodness, the great man was sent shepherding. His early experiences were horrific, starting with having to drive two hundred ewe lambs, just weaned off their mothers, down to their wintering on arable farms near the coast – a distance of one hundred miles, with only one of his father's old dogs to help him. Nowadays he wouldn't manage to do five miles with the traffic we have! Then there were the awful wet beds he had to sleep in with old 'chaff' mattresses, i.e. mattresses filled with chaff from oats threshed probably years before, and never aired, because those living in bothies in those days got scant consideration, as I know to my cost. Then he would tell me about the days when George Grant would take summer grazing for Blackfaced wethers, which yielded big fleeces of wool. Wool was wanted then, and mutton also was eaten with relish. Nowadays one would be better to have a breed like the Wiltshire Down which has no wool, as it costs more to shear the animal than one gets for the fleece. As for mutton, everyone wants lamb, and the only person who eats mutton regularly that I know of (besides myself), is the first character in this book, the Queen Mum – and how good it is with caper sauce.

He had vast stretches of moorland to deal with, a lot of it on Invercauld land around the Devil's Elbow. Not being 'hefted' to the land, i.e. bred on it, he must have found it the devil and all to gather up sheep for the Aboyne sales in October, though he used to say, 'I was fit in those days, Captain'. In all our years together he never called me anything else but 'Captain'. He was a gentleman if ever there was one, and if in his time on earth I'd been asked to take only one person to Buck House or somewhere similar (is there anywhere similar?) I would have taken Robbie, as he never put a foot wrong.

Because he knew the Aboyne area so well, he advised me in his canny way that the sort of Blackfaced ram lambs we were breeding might well suit Aboyne, where the three-day sheep sale was a legendary occasion. In the fifties the Department of Agriculture owned Beechwood and Knocknagael Farms at Inverness and also Wester Aberchalder on the south side of Loch Ness. Between these places they kept stallions, of the Highland Pony breed naturally; bulls – Aberdeen-Angus and Highland, but mostly Beef Shorthorn; and rams – Blackface, Cheviot and Border Leicester. These were available for hire to the crofters on the West Coast and on the Islands at very cheap rates. Changed days now as to the breeds, and for me the change has been for the worse. The Continental breeds of cattle may have done a good job on our lush lowground farms as terminal sires, but they were never meant for the poorer land which at one time used to supply breeding stock for Lowland farmers. As for the Highland Pony stud, it was sold up: and oh! how modern breeders try to hold on now to what they call the 'Department' pedigrees, i.e. something with a Knocknagael blood line in the pony's pedigree.

Also changed are the modern D.O.A.S. inspectors, as all in the old days had been reared on crofts or farms and had no other thoughts in their heads but stock. An example was Duncan Fraser, who after a career of keeping people right with their stock, subsidies etc. retired to a wee farm at Drumnadrochit on Loch Ness side and proceeded to win the suckled calf show and sale at Inverness for pens of five. This he did for four years, and if he had won it a fifth would have won the cup outright; but in this year 1993 that I write, he was bringing in his five calves to trim them for the show and sale when the grim reaper said, 'This night I have need of thee'. What a super finish, what a super stocksman. But the doyen of them all was Jimmie Dean, Duncan's first boss when he was in Inverness and, until his early death, the chief livestock inspector for Scotland. He had a 'great eye for a beast', had been brought up the hard way in Speyside, and helped so many with his advice. But more of him later.

It's never easy to go to a market with stock for the first time and I was more than apprehensive about Aboyne, although the pressure had been relieved by breakfast at 'Briggies' – two large twelve-year-old Macallan Glenlivets plus a plate of bacon and eggs the size of which I had never seen before or since! 'Briggies', i.e. the Cockbridge Hotel, had been Robbie's local for years, and no matter what time of the day or night we arrived the welcome was 'immense' and the biggest problems were (1) how to get them to accept payment and (2) how to get away sober enough to drive the many miles home!

As for the Sale my apprehension was unnecessary, as Jimmie Dean was there buying for the 'Department': our rams were good and he made them a grand trade. Bless you, Jimmie, you were a good friend over many years.

Luckily, not knowing what time we would get away from Aboyne and as we had left Gaskbeg at 4 a.m., I had arranged for us to stay in Strathdon for the night. En route from Aboyne to Strathdon, Robbie suddenly said, 'There's "Bouties", Captain, and I must see my old friend Alex'. 'Bouties' turned out to be the Boulten Stane', a pub in the middle of nowhere which Robert had occasionally visited in his Strathdon days. It just happened that a B.B.C. Scotland Radio team were ensconced there who knew me. Hearing of my success at the sales and knowing I had done a lot of broadcasting, they got me to do a piece about 'the place of sheep in the Highland economy' or something similar, the sort of talk which I've now been doing in one way or another for forty-five years! Anyway, when they said I would be sent a fee Rob and I decided to spend it. Just as I ordered a round, a lovely rubicund face poked round the door of the snuggery with its roaring peat fire, and said: 'Robbie McHardy, for God's sake what are you doing here?' He turned out to be the local baker, who had supplied Rob in his hard-up days on the croft, often on tick, so Robbie, with my help, was determined to repay him. As we drove away, feeling no pain, I saw for the first and only time a baker's van upside down in a ditch with bread rolls, etc. scattered over the surrounding peat. However we rescued the driver and took him back to the pub, where wisely they put him to bed; but as Rob said, 'I doot, Captain, some folk who didn't get their bread in the morning wouldn't think Aboyne Tup Sales was such a great day as we did'.

Robbie served me well at Gaskbeg and with his fantastic honesty, (at a time, in the fifties, when wages were minimal and all too many employees with absentee bosses helped themselves to augment them) when I was offered a Nuffield Scholarship to the U.S.A. for a month in 1951 I had no qualms about leaving him in charge.

When I got back, Creina, my then wife, and I, were offered to buy the farm as tenants. As I had been offered the job as Factor on the Ardkinglas Estate with Michael Noble, and as it gave me the chance of having the first bit of capital ever, we decided, having bought it, to sell. My worry was for the men who had worked so well for me those eight years, first and foremost 'himself'. But I got him a job as shepherd/manager with a neighbour who had been a student of mine.

Rob had a lovely twinkle in his eye, one of his most endearing traits, and both my families loved him dearly. So they should, as he was either nanny, or father confessor, to all six of them. I always remember an occasion when Catriona, brother Philip's daughter, was staying at Gaskbeg and she and my youngest son Donald were laying together on a grass bank; they both had red hair and round faces and nice rosy complexions. Robbie passed with a bale of hay on his back, took one look at 'Tri' as Catriona was known, whom he had never seen before, and said, 'I doot you've been there, Captain'. You were a lovely old rogue, Rob.

After my five years at Ardkinglas, which is what I had contracted to do, I came back to the tenancy of Woodburn near Crieff. However I had been lucky enough to have won a four months' International Wool Secretariat Scholarship, with two months in Australia, one in New Zealand and one in South Africa. It just happened that Robbie's then boss was having to pack up farming because of back trouble (which is better than Bank trouble, an all too common farmers' complaint) so both he and I were delighted to renew our old partnership. As the cottage on Woodburn was only a but-and-ben (two roomed), the McHardys moved into the farmhouse while I was away. Since the farm had been virtually neglected by the previous farmer, Rob's job was more or less to act as custodian until I got back in March 1965, when we both set about making a farm out of it. This culminated in a sale of the cattle stock which grossed £30,000, enough to pay for my two daughters' education at Morrison's Academy, Crieff, and also at

Cambridge and St Andrews University. Oh, I know there are many who boast that they got grants to educate their family, but I would rather boast that I sold Gaskbeg to educate my first four and the Woodburn cows to educate the remaining two.

I finished my scholarship trip in South Africa. I always love to tell the story, which has been in print before, about the end of my stay when, as the I.W.S. seemed to think I had done a good job, they organised for me to have a week's safari in the Kruger Game Reserve. As I'd seen everything worth seeing with brother Wally in Uganda, as you'll have read elsewhere in this book, I was all set to spend my time starting to write my report to the I.W.S., which I knew would be impossible once Rob and I got stuck into farming Woodburn. The night before entering the Park, I stayed with a farming pal who told me that the park had no licence for drink, and one was only allowed to take in two bags; so I packed mine with the excellent wines and sherries produced in South Africa, and also took my travelling radio set as my good friend George Mackie was standing as a Liberal for Caithness and Sutherland, and the polling date was during the time we were on Safari. As March is a bad time to see game there were only five of us on the trip, three old ladies, who seemed to enjoy my free sherry, and a smallish bespectacled gentleman who told me had been putting through a large paint order for his firm with the South African government for their warships, and was taking a rest on his way home. He, since he hadn't been told about the non-licence in the Park, was more than partial to enjoying my supplies! On the night that George Mackie won his seat I was more than usually generous when I poured the drinks, whereupon my travelling companion said, 'My wife doesn't like your Scottish break-away parties, and when she's Prime Minister she'll sort them out.' Needless to say you have now guessed who the person was, none other than Denis Thatcher. However the year was 1964 and the 'Iron Lady', although in the Cabinet as Minister of Education, was unknown to the ordinary citizen like me. When I got home I told the story to Michael Noble, who was then Secretary of State for Scotland, and he said, 'Maggie, as Prime Minister? Her husband must be daft, Ted Heath can't stand her'. How wrong you were on the first count, Michael, but how right you were on the second.

There is a footnote to this story. I was back in Woodburn when Maggie Thatcher, then in opposition, was to visit Perth (which at that time was true blue but I doubt is now) and one of her calls was to be McDonald Fraser's Auction Mart. Roley Fraser, the chairman and old friend of mine, said 'Ben, I want you in your grass skirt' (his name for my kilt) 'to be in the line up to meet Maggie'. I replied, 'Roley, you know I'm a Liberal, but if Denis is coming I'll be there and we'll have free drinks all round!' Sadly he didn't appear, so I never got my own back.

A farm can be run down in a very short number of years but it takes a long time to build it up. This Rob and I tried to do in the happy years we spent together. He was so patient, the sign of a real stocksman, compared with me, as I want everything done yesterday. He was so honest too. I had to leave him time and time again as I went off to factor estates, be secretary to the Aberdeen-Angus Society, broadcast, which I was doing regularly, attend Smithfield meetings in London etc., etc.: but you could leave Rob with everything, yes, even the wife, and both of them loved him dearly. But they were always 'the Missus' or 'Mrs. Coutts' to him, and he would do anything for them, from baby-sitting to hanging out the washing or showing them how to cut up a lamb. Until he retired at the age of sixty-four after a massive heart attack he never divulged to me how he hated killing and butchering the sheep, which like everything else he did to perfection. But as he said, 'It was part of my job, Captain'. No moans, no gripes about 'why not take it to the local slaughterhouse'. Oh! how I wish they bred his sort today. Thorough in his work, a good husband and father, loyal and honest, what more could I, as employer, want? Well, I'll tell you what I got – a friend in whom I could confide and whom I could trust implicitly and whom I miss terribly. After his heart attack I got Robbie and Anne council houses, firstly in Muthill and finally in Comrie, and Rob, on heart pills (like all of us oldies), had another sixteen super years in retirement, but sadly Anne got cancer and died first. I used to visit them once a week and each year took them to Oban from where they went to Iona for their hols. Then Rob was taken and I had the honour of giving the appreciation after, I might say, a Roman Catholic service that might have done for Joe Bloggs or A.N. Other but not my dear friend Robbie.

His great sayings were, if he was putting a sneck on a gate, 'We'll just tie it with binder twine, Captain'. 'Just for fear'. Or when I had been away, whether for a day or months, 'Weel, you're back again'. So I was able to say at the graveyard, which was where the Roman Catholic padre who didn't even know Rob allowed me to speak, that the Lord would greet him, 'You're back again, Robbie, come in and welcome just for fear someone down below tries to get you'.

I salute you, Rob, a great Scot, a great gentleman, a great friend and greatly missed.

MICHAEL NOBLE, LORD GLENKINGLAS, P.C.

M.P. for Argyll, then Secretary of State for Scotland. An employer and friend

I met Michael Noble, later to become Secretary of State for Scotland before being elevated to the peerage, when I was managing Millhills for the late Duncan Stewart where he had the world famous Beef Shorthorn herd. On the Comrie farms of Brae of Fordie and Balmuick Duncan had a top class fold of Highland cattle which Michael came to visit. We just seemed to click, and from then until the day he died we were firm friends, and apart from our politics we had many things in common. Even in our politics, although he was a Tory and I a Liberal, we weren't very far apart. He couldn't stand Maggie Thatcher and her right wing views, and before he died he predicted that the yuppie era would come to a nasty grinding halt. What fun we had together over those forty-odd years, as he was a 'bon viveur' with excellent taste, especially in wine. But going back to the early days of our friendship, at that time he was resuscitating the Dalmally Agricultural Show (which glories in the full name of the Glenorchy and Innishail Horticultural and Agricultural Society). He was its first secretary after the war, and as befits a future Secretary of State for Scotland he made a great job of it. The show was tiny then, and sadly Michael didn't live to see the show of Highland cattle there in 1992 when there were over 100 cattle present, more than at the Royal Highland Show.

Afternoon entertainment has always been a problem at local shows, and Mike and I hit on the idea of having a six-a-side shinty tournament. So we enlisted the help of George Slater, a well known Oban shinty referee, and Archie Black the Dalmally plumber, shinty enthusiast and show committee member. What a success that has been, and in the first year Michael had the satisfaction of seeing his own team, the Ardkinglas Rangers (now sadly defunct), win the cup.

The rightful owner of the Ardkinglas Estate after the war was Sir Donald

Michael Noble

On the left, Michael Noble, later Lord Glenkinglas, seen with his partner and brother John inspecting the 'top' pen of Blackfaced wether lambs at the first 'on farm' sale of sheep in Scotland, organised by the author. The building in the background is now the famous Loch Fyne Oyster Bar

Noble, Bart., but as he was a diplomat and enjoyed his job and living overseas he sold the estate for 'a mess of pottage' to his brothers John and Michael (seen in the photograph with Michael on the left). John was to look after the estate side and Michael the farming enterprise. Johnnie Noble, the present Laird of Ardkinglas, is doing a great job there and good Highland lairds don't grow on every tree. Incidentally Sir Ian Noble, who is a great supporter of all things Gaelic and does so much for Skye, is Sir Donald's son.

After our Dalmally Show liaison Mike and I saw a lot of each other because of our mutual interest in and love of Highland cattle. He just loved looking after his cattle himself, but as he hadn't any practical training in farming and as most of his staff were shepherds who, with one exception (out of ten), looked on the cattle as 'the Laird's hobby', he often had me down from Gaskbeg to help him out with whatever practical problem was bothering him. It was during this period, the fifties, that he endeared himself to the Argyll farmers. Not only was he feeding his cattle, gathering his sheep with his shepherds and attending sheep sales, but also he represented them on committees of the National Farmers Union, the Wool Board etc., so that when eventually he was asked to stand for parliament he had the farming vote to a man. Argyll was then predominantly a farming county, as forestry, fish farming and the 'white settlers', plus all the trappings that go with tourism, were only just starting.

The Highland Cattle Society in the fifties, as now in the nineties, was going through a boom period, and as a result we had a very prestigious membership. It was still the days of the big estates, and bacause of this we had a dinner for the owners and on another night a cattlemen's ceilidh. At the dinner would be the Duke of Argyll, the Duke of Montrose, Lord Trent, Sir Charles MacLean of Duart (later Lord MacLean, Chamberlain to the Queen), Sir Frances Walker of Leys Castle (still one of the best folds in the country), Sir James Denby Roberts of Strathallan, Duncan Stewart of Millhills, Ernest Nelson of Auchnacloich (thank goodness this excellent fold is still going strong), Michael Noble etc., etc., etc., and allowed to the dinner were people like Johnnie Bannerman (what a super character and later Lord Bannerman) and yours truly, because we managed folds for some laird or other. But I was also required at the cattlemen's ceilidh, which I had to M.C., and believe me, as an ex-sergeant major I thought I knew how to control a sing-song in a Sergeant's Mess but then the sergeants drank pints of wishy-washy beer, not bottles of Islay Malt or Old Mull! Anyway there were always two who not only came to the ceilidh but contributed to it, with great acclaim from the 'Jocks'. One was Johnnie Bannerman, who sang beautifully, of course in the Gaelic, and Michael, who had an excellent sweet-toned true voice and who could go through and sing every song in 'Songs of the North', but at the ceilidh would bring the house down by singing a different song of his own making set to a well known tune. The one that comes to mind, after forty years, is set to the tune of the Skye Boat Song, 'Speed Bonnie Boat like a Bird on the Wing', for which his words were:

> Speed bonnie bids, wave your catalogues high,
> Shout if I fail to see,
> Here's a collection of wonderful kye,
> Make your bids fast to me.
> I'll sell them all, short, fat or tall,
> Something to suit each fold,
> Scraggy or thin yet so masculine,
> All have come here to be sold.

Then we would repeat the chorus again and again, as our auctioneer at that time was not, shall we say, in the Premier League!

His ability to mix with all types of people, yes and talk *to* them, not down to them, about things in which they were really interested, was to my mind the greatest of many gifts which he was given.

In 1959 I had the chance of buying Gaskbeg, and as I was a sitting tenant could buy it cheaply and sell it with vacant possesion for very much more. I was not happy with my children's education and wanted to send them away to school. As anyone knows that costs a lot of money, which I didn't have unless I sold the farm. This coincided with Michael having been sent to the House of Commons to represent Argyll, and John his brother complaining that the farming side of the Estate was needing someone to look after it if Mike was to be in London. So they offered me the post of Estate Factor. I went to take up the position in November, 1959, and my three boys went off to boarding schools; and although they complain that it didn't do them any good they have all made their way in the world. When I started working with Michael I found a completely different person from the one I'd worked with in the Highland Cattle Society in my presidential year, when he had been my vice-president. Then he used his excellent brain and his foresight to guide the Society, and helped me tremendously in the financial side as I can't add up two and two! But when he was at home in Cairndow he went into reverse gear and would put off making decisions as long as he could. I, coming from over 1,000 feet above sea-level in Speyside, with its bracing cold climate, was bursting with energy and longing to get my teeth into pulling the Estate together, as it was very fragmented. It was a case of estate versus farm and even shepherd versus shepherd, but I hadn't allowed for the 'West Coast Factor' where everything that should have been done yesterday is put off until tomorrow! It was eventually to get me too, and when I left five years later, and I only promised to stay five years, I was just as willing to sleep in of a morning instead of rushing round waking up shepherds as I did when I first went to Cairndow.

I know now that Michael used his lovely house, Strone, with its garden and the farming side of the Estate as his safety valve. He was extremely knowledgeable about azaleas and rhododendrons and had a greenhouse in which he propogated his young rhodies. Since his family of four girls was being educated in the South and as the family had a pad in London, Michael would often come up for weekends on his own. He would cook for himself as he enjoyed it and was in the 'cordon bleu' class. I never worked with or for anyone who kept such meticulous books as he did. Accounting for the numbers of sheep on any hill farm is far from easy, as there is always what is called a 'black loss' factor. These are sheep that get buried in peat bogs, snow drifts, get washed away, stolen (sometimes, but very seldom, by unscrupulous neighbours) or most likely just got missed at a gathering. Michael had an uncanny gift of knowing what each hirsel (a shepherds' flock and in the 50's numbering about 500) would show, and many a time he upbraided me for bemoaning how many were missing on a certain hirsel at clipping time in July. He would say, 'they'll come in to xyz' (naming a number) by the winter dipping' (November) and he was invariably right.

He had most marvellous ideas which he worked out on paper but sadly many weren't practical and I think this is why we got on so well together; I am no tactician, my feet are too firmly rooted in the soil and I need someone with a brain to make the plans and I'll get them carried out if they are going to make sense. The Cairndow Sheep Dog Trials had been one of his ideas, and today it will be one of the last hill dog trials left in Scotland. What fun they always are, and much more a trial for a hill dog than a flat golf course. But although Mike had run the trials for years and had himself, when he came back to run the farms, gathered the hirsels with the shepherds, he never appreciated how essential the sheep dogs were to the running of the farms. There were in excess of 4,000 ewes to gather, five times per annum, on really rough land rising from sea level to over 3,000 feet, yet he used to argue that so-and-so shepherds had too many dogs and he didn't see why the farm account should pay for their keep (a pittance in the 50's, and some hill shepherds today would give their all to have the kind of dogs we had then!) And yet when we had the staff together, and my army days have taught me the value of letting everyone know what's being planned, Michael would pour drams as if there was no more whisky being distilled!! Strange how we all have our meannesses.

Nowadays when I visit Cairndow I gravitate to the Oyster Bar at Clachan Farm, and when I look round the assembled company, and it's usually nearly full, I always smile to myself as I remember that thirty-odd years ago I was milking the odd Highland cow in the same building, which was then a byre. As I said in a recent broadcast, I'd rather 'tuck in than muck out' as I often took my turn to muck out the dung when the shepherd/cattleman was busy with sheep. One of the first things I did when I went to Ardkinglas was to kick the Highland cows outside, as with their double coats, the long one to shed the water and the fluffy one underneath to keep them warm, they were meant to be outside, and only sweat when 'housed' in a byre. During my five years at Ardkinglas we had two female Championships at the Oban October Sales, when they made figures like 220 guineas – today they would make in excess of 3,000 guineas. Michael just loved his Highlanders, and the sad thing was that in his declining years, when sadly his very heavy smoking brought on emphysema, his then manager made him sell his pedigree fold in a commercial ring, and they made 'sweeties'. If only he had been spared for another five or six years till the tide had turned. Overseas buyers, especially the Germans, had by then realised their worth and the Ardkinglas fold would have made a bomb.

One of the worries of running an estate with a lot of sheep is that at lamb sale time (August/September) and ewe sale time (October) one spent hours and days at sales. Not only did I go, but at least one or two shepherds and possibly the estate lorryman if I didn't drive the vehicle myself. Added to that, the cost of haulage was colossal. The nearest markets were Stirling and Glasgow, as in the fifties Dalmally had not taken off as it has since. I had seen a farm sale in Wales run by a friend of mine, Captain Bennet Evans, which had been a great success. I put the idea to Michael, who jumped at it as we had all the right ingredients, buildings to use as a sale ring and for housing the 'top' lambs so that they would be shown dry, fields to hold the sheep for the days prior to the Sale and lots of lorry and car parking space.

Whenever Michael latched on to the idea his methodical mind started working out which hirsels should be gathered first, where the 'top' lambs should go, then the 'seconds', then the 'shots' (the wee ones) but more importantly, on which date we should hold the Sale, as we wanted to sell the cast ewes as well. We eventually plumped for a date in late September, which was mid way between the lamb sales and ewe sales and one that suited the auctioneers.

I never want to relive that week previous to the Sale again. Timing was all important. If we gathered the hills too early, our grass fields would get over-grazed and dirty and the sheep would look bad, and half the reason for having an 'on farm' sale was that the sheep should look good and fresh. If we left it too late we wouldn't have enough sheep to make a sale. Needless to say, being Argyll it poured non-stop for days, and to make matters worse there was mist to the floor! At last it cleared, and I had to import neighbours to help and put on two squads, one to gather and one to 'sort' the sheep in the fank. Michael was well known in the farming world and in Scotland, so the Sale got great publicity, was a flyer and Michael was over the moon.

Looking back now I realise that had Michael only remained M.P. for Argyll and not become Secretary of State for Scotland we could have done great things together, but sadly as he gave less and less time to farm and estate business his brother, John, got fed up with the partnership and they decided to split it, which coincided with the end of my five-year contract. It's rather ironic that John, who looked after the estate side but was not really interested in the area, unlike Michael, should be followed by his son Johnnie, now living at Ardkinglas, who is doing a first-class job with his oyster bar, fish farm, mussel beds, joinery business etc., etc., in fact being a Highland laird employing a lot of people; whereas Michael's daughters all live in the South and only come up during the 'season', as did the Lairds between the wars.

Scottish history will recount whether M.A.C. Noble was a good Secretary of State or not. When he was speaking at the Annual N.F.U. dinner as Secretary of State and asked for questions, someone asked, 'why do you have a Factor who is a Liberal?' – to which he replied, 'That's nothing, his wife votes Labour!' which at that time was true. But the farming lobby certainly liked him, and although he may not have masterminded the Forth Road Bridge, the Mull Roll-on, Roll-off ferry and the Corfach Pulp Mill, he saw them put into action and completed. The last project gave him great sadness, as he felt it was the answer for the Lochaber district, but because of things out of his control it packed up

The strain of life in the House of Commons, and to a lesser degree the Lords, being a heavy smoker all his life, lack of exercise in his later years plus his enjoyment of a drop of alcohol, which had to be the best, and it was I who guided him from the West Coast malts to the Speyside ones, all took their toll, and we buried Lord Glenkinglas in the family graveyard long before he should have gone.

My lasting impression of him is his keen brain, his sense of humour (he could make disasters seem funny) and his generosity. But sadly, Michael, those two dozen bottles of your best Burgundy which you said you would leave me in your will never materialised – though I certainly drank my share while you lived!

CAPTAIN R.G. MAXWELL, M.C.

Sussex Yeomanry, National Hunt trainer and natural leader of men

Bob Maxwell, (not to be confused with the other Captain Maxwell mentioned in brother Sir Walter's chapter and owner of Pergamon Press) was born in Hawick but never mentioned much to me about his parents, although they can't have been 'skint' as they sent Bob to Harrow.

As Bob had gambling in his blood, his mother being Irish and his father a Scot, I often wondered if his father had been a bookmaker – I was going to say a successful one but I've never known one that wasn't! Although Bob was born in Hawick he never got back to Scotland until he came to see me at Lagganbridge in the fifties, but of that later.

When war broke out and I was a Troop Sergeant Major in the Sussex Yeomanry I was not amused when our Regiment, the 98th (Surrey and Sussex Yeomanry) R.A., was split in two with the first line 98th going to the British Expeditionary Force in France, and the second, the 144th Field, being left at home with a cadre of the first line, of which I was one, in order to train a lot of 'rookies'. I, like all the others of the cadre, little realised how lucky we had been, as most of the 98th were put 'in the bag' for the duration.

When the 144th was formed the Sussex Battery comprised 'A', 'B' and 'C' Troops. I was Troop Sergeant Major of 'B' Troop with a Captain Jimmie Boyd (later killed in action) as Troop Commander and Bob Maxwell as G.P.O. (Gun Position Officer), or second in command of the Troop. What happened in action, and fifty years on it will all have changed, is that the Troop Commander was in the Observation Post (O.P.) up front and relayed the firing orders back to the G.P.O. via that lovely old fashioned system of field telephones and endless telephone wires which the signallers had constantly to repair. At the siege of Keren in Eritrea one of our signallers was awarded the Military Medal, rightly, as he was constantly under enemy fire while mending the lines.

While the regiment was training in Britain, and thanks to two first class regular

Gunner Battery Commanders, Majors Mansergh and Munn, who realised what good material they had to work with, we all got to know each other really well, and it wasn't long before Jim, Bob and I realised we had a common love of horses. I might say it was only after I was commissioned that I would dare to call them by their christian names, even in print!

Jim had always wanted to own a horse, and did for a short time with Noel Cannon. Pre-war Bob had been assistant trainer to 'Towser' Godson, whose son John is doing so well on the flat whereas 'Towser' was mainly a National Hunt trainer. While based at Lewes just prior to the war Bob had got his licence, and had made a brilliant start by training a horse called Brown Cottage, which won two very prestigious races at Sandown, entered for the Welsh Grand National, but unfortunately broke down just beforehand. Lewes, I am told, was a lovely sleepy Sussex town pre-war, and because of the Downs to the north of it was ideal for training horses, which for National Hunt races have to be worked up and down hills to get them fit. I always remember the great Ryan Price saying to me, when I was exercising point-to-point horses that eventually were winners, 'Coutts, make them work downhill, that's what makes them muscle up'.

But back to Bob and Lewes. While he was there Bob fell for and married Winnie Hilder. Winnie had been chased by every horsey man in Sussex because not only was she a stunning blonde with the usual accompaniment of the palest of blue eyes, but she was an outstanding rider and was the person whom Enid Bagnold used as her heroine for 'National Velvet', that famous book about the horse daft girl.

Winnie's father was the local butcher, who bred smashing looking daughters, all of whom married well – or so Winnie thought until Bob went wrong 'with the weakness'. The first of the good looking daughters to marry, I'm told, took her Ayrshire husband, a coal mine owner, to the cleaners! Something that is becoming quite usual today. Winnie's mother, a handsome woman, was also a formidable one, and not only fixed up her daughters' weddings but ruined them, as I was to find out many years after meeting her when I came home wounded in 1942.

When Jimmie, Bob and I got together in 1940, we thought like many that the war would end soon. Yes, all those fifty-four years ago the media had the whip hand and told us this was the case! So we were always discussing during time off what we were going to do, and the theme was always horses. As you will all know one has to enter a horse for a race. When I asked my officers for compassionate leave for a certain gunner, they asked me to state the reason why. My reply was understood by both when I said, 'Sirs, Gunner X has entered his girlfriend for the Pudding Stakes!' I'm told it was recorded in the Battery History as one of the better answers from a mere Sergeant Major.

Bob was, like myself, never too good at Maths, so when we were training in this country he never shone at T.E.W.T.S. (Tactical Exercises without Troops):

Captain R. G. Maxwell

Men of the 'B' Troop 389 Sussex Yeomanry Battery. A photo taken at Dursley, Gloucestershire, just prior to embarkation for the Middle East. Captain Jim Boyd, Troop Commander, is on the right, my character Bob Maxwell, Second in Command, in the middle, and the author, Battery Sergeant Major, on the left

but boy, when we got into action he came into his own. He was a born leader, and even now at the annual Sussex Yeomanry reunion, fifty years on, and we've had a jar or two, chaps who were Sergeants, Bombardiers or Gunners say to me, we would have followed Bob anywhere – yes, to Hell, if he ordered us.

When Bob joined the Battery he had a wonderful batman called Ted, one of his stable lads, who spoke in the real old Sussex tones which I love and which are being lost today. Ted used to talk about someone for whom he worked before Bob and said, 'It was 'im 'ho was in the 'ussars'. Then there was the time when he was telling me about a party that Bob and Winnie had laid on for their owners on a lovely June night on the Sussex Downs, and he said to me, 'there they were, eatin' of a cowcumber sandwitches and a-drinking of a green chateroose'. We don't breed that sort today, more's the pity. They were servants without being servile, and speaking as one who has been a groom and served at table, I can't see why people in this country look down on serving others as compared with other countries. Most of our restaurant service is abysmal to say the least.

The Surrey and Sussex Yeomanry were naturally officered pre-war by people who had a lot of experience of horses, and when we doubled our numbers it was only natural that the older officers recruited friends and relations who were 'horsey' minded. In these days I played the bagpipes and was asked (ordered) to play at an officers mess Burns Night. Although the regiment was formed in Surrey and Sussex there were a lot of officers either with Scottish breeding like Bob, or who had sporting interests in the North. I had been asked to stay on until the end of the evening to play to the departing guests whom, I remember vividly, included the Bishop of Chichester. The reason I remember he was a guest was that the young officers decided to have a steeplechase over the furniture, with the bigger ones as horses and the lighter ones as jockeys. Bob was a horse and Derek Hubbard, later to be clerk of the course at Goodwood, was his 'jock' and they won, but the bumping and boring was horrific and the language turned the air blue. I remember the Bishop turning to our very embarrassed Colonel and saying, 'Well, Colonel, thank you for an excellent dinner. I hope your officers will fight as hard as they went round that steeplechase course tonight and that their obscenities are directed at and understood by the enemy!' I understood that most of the officers were up in front of the Colonel the next morning for a proper wigging.

Bob was so popular in the regiment he was everyone's pal. Probably his especial friend was Tom Bevan, who was Irish and also horse daft, and then we had Rob Barclay of the then famous brewery firm and others with, then, well known brewery tags – Tom Mann of Mann, Crossman and Paulin and Peter Winch of Winch's beer. Since take-overs these are no longer going concerns, but then all these brewers were horsemen.

It was hard to keep the troops happy during that phoney war period before we went overseas, but Bob, although he had no voice worth a damn, always backed me when I said I was organising a sing-song, a dance, a football or rugger match or anything to keep the boys happy. He always turned up, although no speaker – he used to say, 'We of the warrior class are neither speakers or dancing men'! He was certainly no dancer. On one of the few evenings when officers and their wives were invited to our Sergeant's Mess in Brighton, Bob was doing his best to dance with Winnie his wife to the tune 'In the Mood' played by Glenn Miller and his band. Those who remember it will know that it keeps fading away, and as it faded away the first time Bob disengaged himself and made a beeline for the bar, whereupon Winnie, left alone in the middle of the dance floor looking very embarrassed came over to me and asked me to partner her. Was I chuffed? – as she was not only a 'smasher', she was a super dancer. But I got my come-uppance next morning when Bob said in a disdainful tone of voice, 'Sergeant Major, I never thought of you as a dancing man' (with heavy emphasis on the dancing!)

He was a stickler for a good turn out and if things weren't to his liking would say, 'It wouldn't have done for the Duke, Sergeant Major' – as he was a great admirer of the victor of Waterloo, the Duke of Wellington.

On the way out to the Middle East, Sergeant Smith of the Surrey Battery formed a boxing class. I was useless because with my fair skin I bruise horribly, and anyway I never had the 'killer' instinct that one needs to succeed in sport. I of course don't mean literally wanting to kill someone, but having that will to win – nowadays just about at any price. Bob took to boxing like a duck to water, and even though he was drinking a fair amount, from memory he was in the last four of the regimental knock-out tournament.

When we got to Egypt we were sent to the Almaza camp outside Cairo to get all our equipment properly checked over, camouflage painted etc. Bob of course found some pal in the racing world who had emigrated there to train what Bob called 'the little white mice' i.e. the diminutive white or grey Arab horses that raced at the lovely Gezira Racecourse that I was able to attend once I was commissioned. I never felt sore, as some rankers did, that officers were allowed into certain clubs, hotels and restaurants that were not open to rankers. To this day I consider the British Army the finest in the world, though sadly neglected by successive governments, and the officer and ranker system has been part of its backbone. We in the Sergeant's Mess only invited the officers to our mess on very special occasions, and if they got a wee bit fu' and couldn't get down from the rafters where they had been placed by their fellow officers, no mention was ever made of it again – it was a case of 'on parade, on parade; off parade do what you like best'. Of course we didn't admire every officer, but we never showed it, and they can't have admired all of us: but by the time we went into action on the Sudan/Eritrean border we were a damned good fighting unit.

When we went overseas Bob was able to show his leadership. He was completely fearless, one who would never ask a ranker to do anything he wouldn't do himself, and caring for those who didn't have his guts and go. Our Regiment had been lucky, as when we were formed as a second line we were made up by a batch of Cockneys. We were at first horrified that we, the Sussex Yeomanry, with all our proud traditions of being men of the land etc., should be burdened with East End Londoners, but by gosh! how wrong we were. They could think twice as quickly as we could. Blott, my batman, had been a lighterman on the Thames and was a treasure. Nearly all our Number Threes on the guns, who do the gun laying and need to be quick thinking, were Cockneys, whereas our super Yeomen were the lads who could handle the shells and do the physical work. They could drive the 'quads' because they were four wheel drives and thus resembled tractors. Although a lot of us older yeomen were horsemen, a lot (not so much younger) had already got used to the tractor age.

On the way out on the boat and during our stay in Cairo, once I, as Sergeant Major, had sent the troop off on its different tasks, Bob and I would 'talk of the days that once were'. Thank goodness racing has been cleaned up, as he had some horrific stories of the length some trainers would go to to win a race. One horse a trainer had was a shocking bad starter and would swing round at the start or not start at all. The trainer got the horse into a dung midden, up to its belly in the stuff, and then fired a twelve bore gun over its head. After that experience every time that horse was started in a race the trainer, or his aide, went to the starting gate and fired an air pistol and the horse won five races in a row!!

Another story he had was about a farming tenant of a well known landlord. The tenant found that his horse, which was a dead cert, was up against a good horse of the landlord's in the same race. The tenant, who was arguing about a rent rise with the landlord's agent, went into the saddling enclosure and as the trainer of his horse wasn't there told the jockey to lose the race, to which the jockey replied: 'You're not my boss, he's at another meeting with another horse and he's put his shirt on a double that they both win.' And the horse did win, by twenty lengths, but history doesn't relate what happened to the tenant's rent!

At the battle of Keren in Eritrea, a battle which was never given the publicity that future British victories were given because the media was low key then, the Bersegleri and Alpini, both, like our Highland Regiments, full of hill men, fought well. They had the advantage of height, and the hills there are not mere 'Munros' of 3,000 feet but rise to 13,000 feet, so they were always able to command our positions.

We as gunners had to soften them up before the Infantry went in, which they did brilliantly. In front of us was a battalion of the Camerons, and although a Territorial myself, I had to take my hat off to those regulars who fought like tigers. It was for manning one of our observation posts up on top of Cameron Ridge, where there had been a lot of hand to hand fighting, that Bob was awarded his Military Cross. Like all brave men he would never talk about it.

After action in the Tobruk Garrison, where I had my nose blown off which finished my active participation in the war, the Regiment was posted to what was then called Persia, now Iran, and they sat there training, training and more training, with no action. Bob couldn't stand it and volunteered for the Long Range Desert Group, who made such a name for themselves doing those fantastic forays of hundreds of miles in the desert and inflicting all sorts of problems on the German supply line, airports, petrol dumps etc. Bob was just the sort of officer they wanted, 'a cut-me-down Captain' (as these chaps with guts and go were called). I'm sorry to say that in the L.R.D.G., whose members' lives depended on water, and who took two large water bottles per man with them on each foray, Bob's were full of rum! From then on the alcohol started to take over, but he still had fantastic charm and leadership. When he came home to Lewes to start up his training I met his stable lads who would do anything for him – and in his last years of training they did it for no pay, such was his personality.

I was only down once to Lewes post-war to see his stable, which was obviously a happy one, and both Bob and Winnie knew horses. They had a super wee horse called 'Ur' which kept winning in all sorts of company and kept the stable going I would guess. But Bob's gambling instinct got the upper hand. In Lewes in those post war years lived the famous Reece family, the top jump jockeys in the land, and they would be giving Bob 'certainties': but whatever the cause the stable had to be packed up. I always suspect that 'Ma' Hilder didn't help, as Bob wasn't wealthy enough for her liking! Sadly I didn't manage to keep in touch with them from 1945 to 1955, during which period Bob and Winnie went to and came back from Australia. I don't think Winnie had settled, after all even now in the outback it's a pretty chauvinistic country, and then was even more so. But on the plus side they produced their one and only child, Diana, who was to become another good-looker like the Hilders.

I got a phone call in 1955 from Bob asking, 'can I come and stay?' to which of course I was delighted to answer, 'yes'. When I went to Newtonmore station to collect my ex-hero I was shaken when I met a Bob now blotchy faced, still sparsely built, as I was to find he seldom ate, stinking of whisky but still immaculate in his 'British Warm' cavalry great coat. I took him out stalking red deer the next day, and he was amazingly fit for someone who had misused his magnificent physique over the years. He then told me in the following days that his marriage was on the rocks, his mother-in-law had chucked him out, he was broke, and could I employ him? I was very short of cash, but my then wife, Creina, bless her, was very supportive until we began to find bottles in the 'loo' cistern, in her piano, you name it, anywhere but the 'drinks' cupboard, which in the fifties didn't contain much except at Christmas and New Year!! Before I had to harden my heart and tell him he had to go, I had given him the job of being in charge of a wee threshing mill which I had hired as a 'diversification' from my normal farming at Gaskbeg. The mill travelled the area and Bob, ex Captain with an M.C., and a great physical worker, was a 'wow' – that is with the local farmers and crofters, who of course plied him with whisky which I had told them not to do. But when he eventually got 'fu' and turned the mill upside down on the Drumochter pass I had to say, 'Sorry, Bob, enough is enough'.

He got a job as a ghillie with the British Aluminium Company in the famous Corrieyairack Pass and was furious that when he cooked the bacon to perfection, shaking off all the fat, 'those silly b——s shouted, "Where's the goo, Maxwell?"' From there Bob emigrated to Western Canada where he died in a snowstorm in Alberta, certainly, as Bob used to say, 'with the drink taken'.

'Why,' I can hear the reader say, 'did Ben choose Bob Maxwell as one of his great Scottish characters?'

Well, quite simply because pre-war he had all the makings of doing great things in the horse training world, and he was a born leader of men. But the war altered so many people's characters, Bob's for the worse, and in my case, though I say it humbly, because of my time spent on a raft and those years in hospital, for the better.

Bob was, like so few, gifted with charisma, and it's sad he wasted it by his love of gambling and booze. 'There but for the grace of God go I'.

THE RIGHT REVEREND ARCHIE CRAIG M.C., M.A., D.D.

Late Moderator of the General Assembly of the Church of Scotland, and great ecumenist

Of all the people who came and went through the Manse portals of Father's different charges, and there were hundreds, no one had a more lasting effect on the Coutts family than the late Archie Craig. When we were in Milngavie, in the twenties, Archie was padre to Glasgow University, and as he stayed within spitting distance of Glasgow Academy where we boys went to school, it was natural that when one was having to stay behind for music, pipe-band practice, theatricals etc., one went to Archie's for tea.

He was looked after then by his sister, with whom he stayed for far too long, as he married the love of his life far too late for both their good. It was a wonderful marriage that should have produced a family, but it was not to be.

The great man regularly visited our Manse, ostensibly to discuss church matters with Dad, but I suspect more likely to give his beloved Irish Water Spaniel, Toby, some fresh air and real exercise. I was always dog daft and Father and Mother couldn't stand them. I always remember Dad stepping in dog's dirt on a Milngavie pavement and bellowing 'those wretched dogs!'–under his breath he made remarks unbecoming to a man of the cloth which quite shocked me. Anyway, I would take Toby for walks round the Milngavie reservoirs, which allowed Archie to play duets on the piano with Mum, their favourite being *Die Meistersinger*. Dad was not amused as he was left in the garden, which like all manse gardens then was far too big, as were the houses.

Archie came from Kelso and so was rugger daft. They say in the Borders there are three religions: Rugby, Horse-racing and the Church, in that order. I don't know about the middle one, but my subject certainly liked the first and was to do a wonderful job for his church. We boys used to play touch rugby on the spacious lawn in front of the Manse. Just over the wall was an old grouch, an agnostic, a football fanatic with a chip on his shoulder. He had warned us that if our rugger ball was found in his garden again he would keep it. This Saturday, Archie was playing with us and the ball duly sailed over the wall. The future Moderator, who had kicked it, went over to retrieve it, only to be confronted by old Grouch who put a carving knife into the ball in front of his astonished gaze. Previously Archie had always poured scorn on us when we said what an awful neighbour we had. Well! you never heard anything like the conversation that ensued. I wish I had a tape recording of it to play to some of the hierarchy of the Church of Scotland. Archie won every round, and came back with the deflated ball, dusted down his threadbare tweed suit and said, 'That man is evil and could do with a good conversion!'

One of the things we boys loved about the great man was his sense of humour: he had a most infectious laugh which made you laugh with him. I'm glad to say that the last time I saw him a week before his death, though a sadder man after his beloved May's passing, he was still able, when we talked about the old days, to raise the famous laugh. He was a sort of 'Puck': someone that for all his great achievements was always young at heart.

But it wasn't only for his youthfulness and love of life that we admired him, it was also for the advice that he gave us. Strange how one takes it from an outsider but doesn't from one's parents. After all, Dad and Archie were firm friends, and had so much in common that Father was bound to have given us similar advice.

Although he had won an M.C. in the 1914–18 conflict, when we knew him first in the late twenties he was an avid pacifist and used to lecture us about the horrors and wickedness of war. When I joined the Territorials in 1937 both he and Dad were not amused, although when I came back wounded neither could have been kinder or more supportive, real Christians as they were.

Then, of course, it was through Archie that we met the legendary George MacLeod, because they had been pals for years and Archie, although he never got the credit he deserved for it, was in with George in the founding of the Iona Community. Dad too had a small hand in it, as like the other two he had worked in the black spots of unemployment in Glasgow.

All three had terrific gifts of oratory which they used in different ways. I suppose it's a sure sign of old age, but I find it hard to think of ministers today who have the oratory that those three had, as each could hold a meeting or congregation spellbound. I remember once, when back in Melrose on sick leave from Hospital in East Grinstead, hearing George MacLeod do a most brilliant 'huckster' act to raise money for Iona on the Saturday night, and the next day I heard him preach a most moving sermon on 'the widow's mite'. And in all the

The Right Reverend Archie Craig

The Right Reverend Archie Craig M.C., M.A., D.D., after he had rededicated the hexagonal church of Kilmorich at Cairndow, with on his right the resident minister Harry Thomson and behind him the author

years that I have attended the Church of Scotland Assembly, how the art of debate has diminished. I suppose one must put it down to the fact that those three, and their generation, spent years of their lives studying and reading, yes, and reading really serious stuff. I know Father was fantastically well read and could quote, and often did in his sermons, from Greek, Latin, any famous authors, you name it; whereas nowadays with radio and T.V. and the hectic pace of life, many young ministers never get the time or the inclination to study as did their forebears.

Being a rugby-daft family you can imagine the reaction among us boys when one Sunday the road beside Dad's church in Milngavie had three or four cars parked in it with 'KS' registration number plates. We knew those letters stood for Roxburghshire, so that meant it had to be a vacancy committee from one of the churches in that rugby-playing county – what excitement! It transpired that Hugh Walker, then headmaster of the famous Border preparatory school, St Mary's, Melrose, who had been a prisoner of war with Archie, had approached him to see if he could recommend a minister who was good with the young, as the church they attended had a vacancy. The result was a call to Father from St Aidan's Church, Melrose. I must say, although I'm his son, Dad was the ideal choice. To this day I meet Borderers of my vintage who remember how much they enjoyed Dad's children's sermons, and that's a long time ago. Sadly, many of them no longer have Kirk leanings, because they say they no longer get the simple message that they got from Dad. But, back to Milngavie, we had all enjoyed being there, especially Mother, who as usual had been, with her striking good looks and strong character, the 'Queen Bee' of all sorts of things, the Amateur Opera Society, Women's Guilds, Chairwoman of the Board of Governors of a private kindergarten etc.

With regard to the kindergarten, they appointed a very good looking teacher, one Ros Barron, who hailed from the South West of England but had relations who were well known Blackfaced tup breeders at High Craigton just outside Milngavie. Ros was a faithful attender at St Luke's, Dad's church. Dad was a great believer that congregations needed a change of voice every now and then, how right he was, so from time to time he exchanged pulpits with someone. The visiting minister always stayed at the Manse, and on the occasion that a certain very shy young minister from Aberdeen was preaching Mum asked Ros to supper to make up the party. The young minister was one Jim Stewart, later to become one of the most famous Scottish preachers of my time and like Archie a famous Moderator. Some months later Ros asked Mum where she could find a tartan rug, whereupon Mum replied, 'Would you be wanting Stewart tartan by any chance?' Shrewd old girl she was, as father married them the next year.

Jim Stewart of course went on to be a Professor, one of the greatest preachers in my time and an outstanding Moderator. But as to his preaching, he had a lot to thank dear Ros for, as before they married she would sit, incognito, wherever he was preaching and give him marks out of one hundred. After he was finished she would hand them to him and she always kept the marks low!

Another visiting minister I remember well, but will never divulge his name. He came from the Islands and was a fantastic preacher, but obviously knowing he would have a 'dry' supper with us he had popped a bottle of something worthwhile in his travelling bag. As a result, two things happened that night I will never forget. The first being that, whether he was naturally a slow eater or whether it was because 'he had the dram taken', I know not, but he had been talking to Mum and when he finished his fish – it was the days of one course followed by scones, pancakes etc. – she looked round and saw, as she said, 'a stricken battlefield'. Every, but every, plate had been cleared by us starving boys! History does not relate how she refilled the plates, as we were on short rations in those days, and we really looked forward to visitors coming as we got 'goodies' instead of the monotonous 'jelly pieces'. but the real reason brother Wally and I remember this famous preacher was when Mother said what a marvellous sermon he had preached, and how much home-work it must have taken etc., to which he replied in that lovely lilting West Coast accent, 'Och, the sermons are easy – it's the prayers, the prayers is the boggers'. Complete collapse of the junior Coutts and complete embarrassment for mother.

But back to Milngavie and the call to Father from St Aidan's Church. Dad loved youth and had a gift of getting on with them, so the call was right up his street. He also loved the Borders, having got to know them in his first charge in Coldstream. But he was hopeless with money matters, and Mother was NOT amused that he was going to take a drop in salary, but as Dad always said, the Ministry should be for those who felt the calling, not for those who thought about the rewards.

So off we went to Melrose, where we were to see a lot more of Archie because of Dad's chaplaincy at St Mary's, and Archie's friendship with Hugh Walker. What wonderful crack those three used to have. It was the days before T.V. and only middling 'wireless' reception and discussion then was an art sadly missing in so many homes today. How I wish I had listened to those pearls of wisdom that those three wise men dropped, but at that age all I thought about was farming, rugger and of course the fair sex.

With regard to the rugger, the first Saturday after we had 'flitted', I was sent to Galashiels by Mother, on a double decker bus, for something obscure she couldn't get in Melrose. On the way back I was sitting on the top, and that was open to the skies in those days, so I had that wonderful view of the Tweed Valley with its incomparable mixture of trees that were changing colour as it was autumn. While I was enjoying the view a burly wee red-headed boy wearing a Gala Academy blazer came bursting up the stairs and said, 'Are you one of the Coutts boys?' and when I said yes he said, 'How many of you play rugger?' to which I answered 'Four'. 'Great,' he said, 'I played for Gala Academy this morning and I'm playing for Melrose 2nd XV this afternoon and we're a couple of players short, any chance of one of you playing?' The red-headed laddie was none other than the legendary Charlie Drummond, who remained a pal of mine until his untimely death. I played for Melrose 2nd XV that afternoon at Walkerburn, and will never forget that as the latest joined member I had to retrieve the ball whenever it landed in the River Tweed. As it was the days of the leather ball it got more and more heavy for the goal-kickers and I got wetter and wetter!

Charlie and I were Sergeant Majors in Cairo together and shared many happy times, including singing in the Church of Scotland choir. This, I suspect, had quite a bit to do with the fact that the Scottish Hospital nurses supplied most of the choir! After the war our paths diverged as, because of my wound, my rugby-playing days were finished, although we did both play for a British Army team versus the New Zealanders while in Cairo. Charlie went on to play for Scotland many times and to become an illustrious President of the Scottish Rugby Union.

Then suddenly after years when we hadn't seen much of each other we saw quite a lot of each other again, because Charlie, as Manager of the Royal Bank in Cupar, took on the secretaryship of the Fife Agricultural Show. From then on we met bi-annually and talked endlessly of the 'days that once were'.

There is no doubt that, thanks to Archie Craig, Melrose was father's happiest charge, and mother as usual got into all sorts of activities, one of them being the organisation of the soup-kitchen/canteen during the war. Sadly for them and for Melrose the Poles were stationed there for far too long. I say sadly, because the Poles were longing to fight the people who had over-run their homeland, and for Melrose it was sad because the local regiment, the King's Own Scottish Borderers, had already been in action and they had their dead and wounded. After I was wounded, Mum, like many another in the town, was not as Christian to those poor lost foreigners as she should have been. She always said that no matter what was on the menu the Poles always said 'Feesh and cheeps' – these were the only words of English they had.

When I came back walking wounded, who should be staying at the Manse but A.C.Craig, and we used to take long walks along the Tweed together and back through the town. As my face was still in bandages, and looking much worse than it really was, as by that time I had had some twenty of my twenty five operations, people used to stop me in the street and ask after my health. Although I am shy – something which no one ever believes – I enjoy a good crack, so often our journey took quite a long time. Archie himself, even then, was well-known by those with Kirk connections. After one of those walks he said to me, 'What are you going to do when you're demobbed?' To which I replied: 'Farm'. Though how in the world I thought I was going to achieve that, with my lack of experience and lack of capital! (Conceit I suppose.) 'Did you ever think of the Ministry, Ben?' he said, 'because you seem to have the common touch and you've had the sort of experiences that help a man in the pulpit, as I found after the First World War'.

Well, I must say, coming from someone of his standing this set me thinking. So one night when Mum was out at one of her various committees I tackled Dad about the possibility of me joining the Church. His answer was typical. 'My dear boy, you couldn't even pass your first-year Vet exams and you had two goes at them, how do you think you can master Hebrew and Greek? Anyway, the Church of Scotland desperately needs laymen as Presbyterians, they depend on the laity.' Well, Dad, I've done my best and have preached on many occasions, including once in St Giles, which was a colossal thrill. But it's thanks to the voice you gave us that the Coutts family have been in demand as public speakers and broadcasters.

There were some years that I didn't see much of the great A.C.C., as I went North and he climbed higher and higher in Church affairs. He was outstanding as a member of the World Council of Churches. How he organised the first visit of the Moderator of the Church of Scotland to Rome and his meeting with the Pope I'll never know, but it got world wide news coverage and they obviously hit it off from the word go. The apocryphal story of their parting was that Archie said 'So long, Pope John', and the Pope replied 'Arrivederci, Erchie'.

Sadly, as with so many high ranking committees, there were personality clashes. Archie just couldn't stand them and resigned gracefully, but what a loss he was to the ecumenical movement. Here we are all those years on with fewer and fewer people attending regular Sunday worship, and yet certain members at the top of all denominations stick to their own dogmas and are unwilling to give an inch to amalgamate the different branches of Christ's Church. Sad, sad.

When I went to be Factor for Michael Noble at Cairdow I naturally attended the local lovely wee, hexagonal Church there. The Parish was called that of Kilmorich, an equally lovely name, I always thought. We were linked with Lochgoilhead, and had a minister with whom I got on very well, although I always said he preached for too long. Sometimes I used to point, very obviously, at my watch, much to his annoyance. But notwithstanding that we got on like a house on fire and both decided the Church needed re-decorating. The pews needed setting further apart as no one my size could sit in them comfortably, and the outside of the Church was literally crumbling – not helped by the hundred-inch annual rainfall in that area. But as with all such Church projects, where was the money to come from? Michael's wife Ann, although a Jew, was a regular attender of the Kirk. As she was a great organiser I approached her to help me run a garden fête in the lovely Ardkinglas grounds.

It was a 'wow', even if I, with scant knowledge of trees, announced on the notice of the fête that the Arboretum would be in full flower. Ardkinglas has the tallest tree in Scotland and always advertises its famous Arboretum when the gardens are open in the spring – I wrongly thought this Arboretum was a type of tree and flowered like their famous Azaleas and Rhododendrons!

Jack Maclay was Secretary of State for Scotland and a keen churchman. As he was a friend of Michael's we got him to open the fête. The event was a great success and we made 'enough and to spare', as the Bible says, to do up the Church properly. We were lucky in the fact that there was a good architect in Lochgoilhead who was a member of the congregation: he not only gave his services free but used light blues and pinks in the interior decoration instead of that awful dark brown, so often seen in Scottish churches, which I call 'Scots Kirk Dung colour'

The obvious person to ask to re-dedicate the Church was the Moderator, and I was in luck as Archie said he would oblige and made a rare job of it too.

When he retired he and May went to live in Doune, but he remained much in demand in pulpits up and down the country. On an occasion before that he had the Coutts family all crying when he made a moving tribute to his old friend, our father.

Sadly, May lost her memory and became increasingly less mobile. This took a lot out of the great man both mentally and physically as he had to lift her into and out of her bed, her wheel-chair etc. But he never lost his love of life or his interest in other people's lives, nor, thank the Lord, his sense of humour. My lasting memory of this man who had a great effect on my life is of him throwing back his head with laughter and at the same time smacking his knees with pleasure.

I always thought he got scant praise for the work he did for the Church, but many, like me, will always thank God for the life of this Great Scot.

DUNCAN FISHER FERGUSON

Late Manager of Glenartney Estate for Drummond Estates, one of a dying breed of practical estate managers

Fisher, named after his mother's family from Balquhidder, was a namely person in so many areas. In his home district of Upper Strathearn he was known among the clay pigeon shooting circle, for not only had he represented Scotland on many occasions, but he was familiar throughout the land just as the character he was to anyone who could handle a gun. Then, among the Blackfaced Tup fraternity, a fairly closed shop I might say, they always loved to see Fisher at their sales. Although not the tops price-wise, like Lanark and Newton Stewart, the sales in Perth, Stirling, Oban and Dalmally were all important to the flockmasters in Argyll and the North, especially in the Islands before the advent of roll-on, roll-off ferries. Before and just after the war those sales were not only essential for the flockmasters in each area, but also an occasion for a 'spree', and no one was better at organising a spree than this character. Then to the cattle side of his managing job he always brought a bit of charisma.

Killin was always noted for its suckled (i.e. six month old) calf sale in September. As well as attracting genuine hill calves, for which it was famous, like many markets it included less authentic stock. Some arable farmers, myself included, jumped on the bandwagon and sold our calves there. Fisher, not to be outdone, went into the ring and sprinkled heather on the backs of his calves, announcing to all and sundry, 'You can see these are genuine hill calves, they still have the heather on their backs!'

But probably it would be for his ability to shoot and manage grouse that he was most universally known. His boss the Earl of Ancaster, Colonel Bill Stirling of Keir and Commander Muir of Braco Castle, all excellent shots themselves, used to ask Fisher to make up their party if they wanted to have a respectable 'bag'. I get increasingly fed up with the do-gooders who disrupt country sports, but especially grouse shooting. I would like one of their number to stand in a grouse butt and take on a covey coming down wind at sixty miles per hour. If they hit one, which I think unlikely, all they would do is wound the bird, which would die a lingering death. All my life I've seen the grouse population rise and fall, and thank goodness they can't be reared artificially as are the majority of pheasants today. Bad hatchings because of bad spring weather, worm infestation, the dreaded tick, bad heather burning management (since grouse only feed on young heather) all have an effect on the grouse population, which makes them a very special gamebird as far as I'm concerned. Fisher felt this too, and after my days as a ponyman in Glenartney where his father was my boss, I came back from the war to factor some well known Highland estates and 'Fish', as I called him, and I had many good-going discussions, and arguments, about grouse management and also deer management.

There are only a handful of people that I have known who were good shots with gun and rifle. Fisher was one, Ewan Ormiston of Newtonmore another, Pat Wilson of Glenalmond and Ross-shire three, and lastly Angus McKillop, head stalker at Glenkinglass, Argyll, when I took over the factorship of that estate in 1961.

McKillop, to digress slightly, was an Atholl man and had been in the Scottish Horse in the First World War. He was an unknown character in Argyll, and when he first went to the local clay pigeon shoot he was shunned not only because he was a total stranger but also because he had an ancient damascus-barreled twelve bore hammer gun which, when he loaded it, everyone could see (and hear) that the stock and barrels were loosely put together. As one observer said to me years later, 'It was the sort of gun that could shoot round corners'. But the silent laughter was soon stifled when old Angus blew every clay pigeon into dust. He won the cup and continued to be 'in the money' every year until he retired to his beloved Atholl. He and I got on well together because of our war service, and we both called a spade a spade. I remember well when I took on the Factor's job first and went up Loch Etive in the mail boat which sailed Monday, Wednesday and Friday, then up the old track from Ardmaddy to Glenkinglass Lodge, a distance of six miles. I realised then that old Mac was another, like myself and so many hill men, who despises modern transport and treats it accordingly. And so it transpired, as round the Lodge and his cottage there was an assortment of clapped-out vehicles which today would be collectors' pieces and worth a bit of money. I made Mac show me round all the buildings and he was rather reticent about letting me into one. When we got in, the place was jam-packed with deer skins, and as it was May month and out of the shooting season I wondered why, but I was soon to find out. Every time I visited, which was normally once a month, I had a meal with old Mac and his housekeeper, and I never was offered anything but venison whether it was in or out of season! He ate it like one does corn on the cob, taking it up in his two hands and applying

Duncan Fisher Ferguson

Duncan Fisher Ferguson, the third generation of his family to manage the Glenartney Estate for the Ancasters. A first class shot, he is seen here with the last stag that he stalked before retirement, a 'Royal' (12 pointer) no less. Practical hill estate managers of his type are sadly thin on the ground nowadays himself to it like someone with a mouth organ! And how it disappeared. I've never seen anyone who could put away so much in such a short time! He was a lovely character, a loyal servant and honest too, and if anyone reading this thinks that he couldn't be honest because he ate venison all year round they'd be wrong, because the forest was grossly overstocked and he was doing it a favour!

Fisher of course knew McKillop through their hobby of clay pigeon shooting. When I was working in Glenartney as a boy the clay pigeon shoots were one of the main recreations for keepers, stalkers and ghillies, and there was great rivalry between teams Glenartney, Comrie, Killin and Luib. All had good teams in the thirties.

In my schoolboy days and up until I was wounded I played the pipes, and 'Fish' was determined that I should pipe the Glenartney team on to the field at Luib, so I was highly honoured to be taken up there in his old 'model T' Ford. 'That was the day that was.' Fisher's father, old John, had ordered Fish not to drink as he was the driver. This was not for fear of being had up for drunk driving, as the law was not in being then (and anyway the local bobbies were all pals of the Fergusons), but because old Ferguson didn't want to land in the ditch, an all too common occurrence then! The Glenartney team won the Cup, and so the celebrations started in the Luib Hotel run by that wonderful couple the Stewarts. What's happened to our hoteliers in Scotland? With all too few exceptions we don't have the like of the Stewarts. What a welcome one got, what courtesy they showed. As for their food – real porridge, real cream from their own cow, real eggs from hens that had scraped in the midden, scones and pancakes etc with home made butter and home made jam to go with them. Oh! I could wax even more lyrical, but what a wonderful couple they were. After the war when I was managing Ben Challum Estate, part of which was behind Killin and part at Crianlarich and Tyndrum, I often popped in to see the Stewarts.

Since my first visit to their Hotel as a boy I had learnt the pleasures of 'a wee dram'. Dear Mrs Stewart used to say 'I'll just go to the dispense and get you a "refresh", Captain Coutts', and being a complete teetotaller she always poured a 'wheecher'! I always like teetotallers pouring drinks, they have no idea of amounts and pour large ones!

On the famous night when Glenartney won the Cup we had to stop at every hostelry on the way home. Fish's father little realised that every time his son had ordered a glass of milk it contained at least a large whisky, if not more! There were stopovers at Lochearnhead, where mine host Willie Cameron was so super, then at the Drummond Arms in St Fillans where the owner was Mr Campbell, who always turned out as if it was the Ritz and always introduced Miss Urquhart (who ran the place impeccably) as 'my manageress', but methinks there was more to it than that!! Then it was the Royal at Comrie. Of course the Cup had to be produced each time, and the two things I've learnt about drinking out of a cup are (a) you don't know how much you're drinking and (b) it's usually gut rot! But after the Comrie stop I was ordered to take over the driving. All I can say is, thank goodness there was practically no traffic on the road, and Tom McGlashan, of whom more later, was the local Bobbie. Those reading my ramblings who are old enough will remember that the old 'model T' Fords had a clutch-cum-brake on one pedal which wasn't the easiest for a beginner. Luckily the vehicle was not heavily loaded, because if it was, when one came to a steep hill, and there was one in the Glen, one had to go into reverse as that gear had a lower ratio than first! Anyway, I got them home safely and cemented a friendship with the Ferguson family and their Fisher relations which sadly went a wee bit off the rails when Fisher became less of his 'old and bold' self.

Going back to the Drummond Arms Hotel, St Fillans was where the Coutts family were brought up. Our house was requisitioned for the 'duration' so on one occasion Mum and Dad went back to see everything was O.K. and stayed in the Hotel. A peppery old Colonel of the First World War was staying there permanently, who had claimed a seat beside the roaring log fire Miss Urquhart put on each evening. Also staying when Mum and Dad were there was a couple obviously on honeymoon. One evening (after his second large pink gin) the Colonel saw the young lad of the couple come in looking very flushed, and without his 'better-half'. Much to my parents' embarrassment he said in an all too loud whisper, 'Enter the male bird in full breeding plumage'!

Then of course Tom McGlashan, the Comrie Bobbie, was what police were all about in the old days. Because he had diabetes he was, wisely, left in Comrie for most of his tour of duty. As laddies we were in awe of him. He was six foot plus, wearing blue breeches and wonderfully rolled puttees – one word from him and a clip over the ear and you bolted home like a frightened rabbit! I remember well going to the Comrie 'Flambeaux' parade back in the early thirties (this is now famous Scotland wide). I and my pal had rockets we wanted to set off, which had cost us more than we could afford. Stupidly we set them off in Comrie Square, where everything happens at New Year, beside a Morris Cowley car with a canvas hood. Why we didn't face them in the direction of the sky I will never know but all I do know is they ended up on the canvas hood of the Morris, fizzing away and certainly not going skyward, and the next thing I knew was old Tom tapping my shoulder and saying 'I'm going to tell your faither about you, laddie'. In these days that was enough, I was on my bike and off to St Fillans like greased lightning. I probably have never covered that five miles I did to St Fillans as fast, terrified lest Father found out!!

But those were the days of 'Bobbies on the Beat' which we are trying to get back to. For many different reasons this seems hard to achieve. Could it be that T.V., for all its marvellous plusses, has had a minus effect on teenagers when it shows films denigrating the police? Or have some of the police by their actions brought this on themselves? I wouldn't know but I do know in the thirties the

Force was more highly regarded and respected. Talking of respect I always remember Tom Dow of Caroglen, Glenlednock, telling me about the high regard he had for the 'polis'.

Tom was legendary in the area as he had 'bairned' seventeen children. They say 'it's a wise man that knows his father' but as all were red headed like Tom they couldn't deny their parentage, and what a super lot they were as they all made good. Tom, like many at that time before and after the war, made the extra wee bit of ready cash by helping at the grouse shooting. As an assistant keeper he would get his 'tip' at the end of the season. Having received it he set off down Glenlednock in his trap drawn by his Highland pony. Shopping completed, Tom went to meet his pals in the Royal, who had all received their 'tips' from the 'guns' who came from South of the border. In those lean thirties money for drams was hard to come by. So a good time was had by all!

Come the end of the 'pairty' and Tom clambered into his trap, and the other Tom (McGlashan the local Bobbie) slapped the horse on the rump and said, 'Take him home'. Changed days indeed! What neither of the Toms knew was that the Lednock was in flood, and when they got to the ford which one has to cross to get to Caroglen the pony stopped and wouldn't budge an inch. When Tom woke out of his drugged sleep and saw the Lednock in full spate he realised what a lucky man he was. He said to me later, 'I'll never have any breed but a Highland pony to take me home, they have more sense than I have'. He admitted that he had tried to force the pony to cross the ford but it had stubbornly refused.

In the thirties the village of Comrie was very dependent on the surrounding estates for seasonal employment, especially in August and September when beaters were required for the different estates in upper Strathearn. The estate Glenartney that Fisher's father and then Fish managed would be the largest and also had the most grouse. In those days there was also a vast number of 'white' hill hares which I always think make the best soup I know. Every Christmas time Comrie was awash with hares which were distributed by the Estate as Christmas boxes. Game was so plentiful for those who could afford it, that I remember one year the Glenartney lorry, packed with hares and ice from the local fishmonger, was sent all the way to Manchester as buyers for them couldn't be found in Scotland! Nowadays countries in Europe fall over themselves to procure Scottish game and send lorries to fetch them as they do with our shellfish also. I often wonder if those who oppose the control of vermin realise what they are doing to the game population which is a terrific money spinner for our rural areas. When I was a boy, although vermin were controlled, we had eagles, buzzards, kestrels, sparrow hawks, hoodie crows, ravens etc., but nothing like as many as we have today, and if we're not careful we'll land up like France where you are lucky if you see a single blackbird!

Dunira, one of the estates like Caroglen between Comrie and St Fillans, was owned by W. Gilchrist McBeth. 'Gillie', as we called him behind his back, had inherited a fortune from his father who built ships on the Clyde during the First World War. 'Clyde built' was a trademark to be reckoned with in those days. Gillie was more than good to the district, and unlike many sportsmen today who take a shooting lodge and have all their food and drink sent from Fortnum and Mason's or wherever, Gillie used the Comrie shops. He had a tremendous labour force, all local where possible, including the seventeen Dow children who all started illustrious careers in different jobs on the estate.

One who was not local was the professional cricket/golf coach who was imported from Yorkshire for the summer to give sports lessons to the locals. I was proud to wear a Dunira Cricket Club cap and was very annoyed when it got lost in one of my many moves. The needle match was against Comrie where the great Sir George Dundas, who played until he was a ripe old age, held sway. Comrie is still going very strong but sadly Dunira Cricket Club has been defunct since the war, when we all had to 'dig for victory' and the cricket pitch and golf course were ploughed up.

But one thing remains to Gillie's memory that is better than any gravestone, and that is the beech hedge which is still beautifully trimmed each year. Most people who have motored in Perthshire will have seen it and admired it, but few will know about its origin. During the mass unemployment in the late twenties and early thirties, W.G. McBeth had his own station erected on the Crieff-Balquhidder railway line owned by the L.M.S. (London, Midland and Scottish Railways). The station is now a very attractive house with its red tiles and very obvious signal box. Into his station W.G. McB. had a trainload of unemployed Glasgow ship workers discharged every day, and they transformed the run-down Dunira Estate into one that was a joy to behold. Among the many tasks they performed was planting the beech hedge which is a lasting memorial to the good 'Gillie' did for the district.

Sadly Mrs McBeth was not as interested in the locals as was her husband, in fact she could be damned awkward. I remember well Joe Smith, who was the farm manager there in the thirties, telling me that he had to have two lots of hens, Rhode Island Reds which laid brown eggs and White Wyandottes that laid white ones, as whichever he produced she always wanted the other colour! The gardener too got so fed up moving things in the garden to please 'madam' that he planted everything in pots that could easily be transplanted! And the head keeper was not amused when he had to have dog collars made in the McBeth tartan for all his Black Labradors. The keepers too had to appear at each shoot adorned with a McBeth tie (which to my way of thinking is not the nicest of the tartans as it has too much blue in it).

But Gillie did a great job for that district in those real depression years of the thirties. I, among many others, have a lot to thank him for, as it was helping as a laddie to show his Highland ponies that fired me with a love for the breed and its breeders, and my love of local shows as a result. So, speaking as ex-Chairman and now Vice President of the Grantown, Dalmally and Braco Shows, you probably have more to answer for than you thought, W.G. McB., and from me thanks. From the committees of those shows you would probably get the comment 'damn your cotton socks, why on earth did you get him interested in showing!'

Fisher too was keen on shows, their camaraderie and competitiveness suited him well. There was the famous occasion when the Perth Tories decided t o run a livestock auction in aid of their funds, and as the then Sir Alec Douglas Home was their M.P., and what a popular one he was, he was asked to contribute. This he did by donating a Highland cow which then made a hundred or two – now she would make thousands! Fish bought her for Glenartney, much to the derision of the employees on that estate and also many worthies in the district. But Fisher was to have the last laugh, as the cow produced a heifer calf and when she was a yearling I took her down to Woodburn, got her halter-broken and properly handled, kept her six months on good feed and then took her to the Oban October Sales, where she won her class and made twice as much as her mother had cost the Estate!

As modern farming techniques have progressed, not all for the better in my opinion, there are fewer Fishers about. When I was a boy all the big hill estates were managed by practical men who knew how to handle their workers because they had done the job themselves. All the characters I've written about who were or are responsible for staff wouldn't ask anyone to do a job they themselves couldn't do. And the estate managers of yore were stocksmen who knew what a good beast looked like and the type that would suit their land. The 'books' were kept by a firm of lawyers or a bank, in the days when banks did much more for you than they seem to want to do today! One of these lawyers was nicknamed 'Swicky Stewart' and it was the most unfair nickname that was ever given to any man, as he was my Secretary when I was President of the Highland Cattle Society and a more honest man you couldn't find.

But nowadays the farming side of estates is all too often run by firms of Land Agents or Consultants from the larger cities, and there is seldom a 'Fisher' on the ground to look after the day to day management. As it happens I know one or two estates which still employ a 'Fisher' type of person, and strangely enough their stock consistently makes top prices at the markets, their deer stocks haven't got out of hand and they always seem to have some grouse when other moors are barren.

Fisher retired to St Fillans where his old friend 'Baldie' McNaughton, although older and for all his life a keeper under Fisher, brought him his daily paper and lit his fire. I used to go up once a week and see them and 'the crack about the old times was guid'. It's so easy for those of us who lived pre-war to talk of the 'good old days', but Baldie, Fisher and I, sitting in a centrally heated room with a dram in our hands which Baldie and I couldn't afford pre-war, could well remember the other side of the coin – those damp bothy beds, those long, long hours when wages were small, those bitterly cold days when one's hands were so stiff with cold one couldn't connect the strap with the buckle to secure the hinds on the deer saddle. Oh! and lots, lots more.

But with Fisher's death in 1993 at the age of eighty, his generation of hill estate managers is dying out. I hope the 'new entry', as the hunting fraternity would call them, can do their job as honestly and well, will treat their staff as well, will shoot as well, will judge stock as well, and will enjoy life as well as did Fisher – but 'I hae ma doots'.

JIMMIE DEAN

Department of Agriculture for Scotland Chief Livestock Inspector, Northern Area based on Inverness

Jimmie was one of the outstanding stocksmen that I have had the honour to know well. He was one of the last of a dying breed who knew about stock, and had had a very hard upbringing, some of which had done him nothing but good in his chosen profession. I have nothing against the modern livestock inspectors, but because of the changes in our farming practices with mechanical aids and modern technology there is no way that they could have the same apprenticeship as did Jimmie. He was the only Scotsman that I knew who had killed cattle for his father's butcher's shop by pole-axeing them. When I was in the Argentine I saw it being done but it had been stopped in this country long before I started farming. I don't think the folk farming in the North of Scotland ever realised how much good he did for the livestock in that vast stock rearing area.

Knocknagael was a farm just outside Inverness owned by the Department of Agriculture for Scotland. This farm used to have a stud of Highland ponies second to none in the land, in fact to this day Knocknagael breeding is eagerly sought after. Also this farm was the centre from which Blackfaced and Cheviot rams bought by the D.O.A.S. were hired out to the crofters in the Highlands and Islands for ridiculously low rents; and how they improved the sheep stocks, which otherwise would have had rams used whose only value was that they were the cheapest available! Bulls too were bought by Jimmie and his gang of subordinates, and in the forties and fifties the bulls were either Beef Shorthorn, Aberdeen Angus or Highland. Sadly today the demand from the Islanders has been for Continental sires, but to my way of thinking these are not the type for the Highlands and Islands where replacement females should be bred.

But in all my dealings with stocksmen no one knew the Islanders' needs better

Jimmie Dean's Ponies

From left to right, three great Highland Pony stallions: Glenmuide, Strathspey and Ben Cleuch, which have all had a lasting influence on the breed. They were part of the famous Department of Agriculture stud at Beechwood, Inverness, which Jimmie Dean managed so well for so many years. Many native breeds and breeders of ponies, cattle and sheep are in his debt for the job he did there

than Jimmie, and I believe had he been in charge today the cattle breeding policy in the Islands would have been different. Having said that I am in no way casting aspersions on today's D.O.A.S. inspectors, but Jimmie was such a strong personality, and in his day, just after the war when farming was wanted, he had the chiefs at St Andrew's House (which he called the Scottish Kremlin!) in the palm of his hand. The first time Jimmie and I were together was going to Uist where he had put my name forward to judge the Highland cattle. I had met him many times before when I managed the Millhill's herd of Beef Shorthorns and the Balmuick and Brae of Fordie Highland Cattle Folds, but then we had both been 'on duty' and on our best behaviour. Going out to Uist we were 'off duty' and enjoying more than one or two drams, as it was blowing a force nine gale and the boat was wallowing as only the old MacBrayne boats could. The skipper was the legendary 'Squeaky' Robertson, so called because of his high pitched voice. In the morning when berthing in Lochboisdale a lady passenger went up to 'Squeaky' and said, 'Captain Robertson, but for you and the Lord we wouldn't be here this morning.' To which he replies in his inimitable voice, 'Two good men!'

That day with Jimmie was memorable, as everyone knew him. We were told to be outside the Loch Boisdale Hotel at 9 a.m., and as I recounted in *Bothy to Big Ben* Jimmie's Departmental Inspector came for us an hour later. 'When the Lord made time he made plenty of it' is the usual West Coast excuse when they're late!!

That day was one of the highlights of my judging career. Good classes of cattle, not led, not overfed, everyone having all the time in the world. (As our boat didn't leave until next morning and the days are long in the Western Isles in summer, we too as judges were lulled into that wonderful feeling that 'Manyana' to the Spanish is a sense of 'ourgency' to a West Coaster.) After judging I had to accompany Jimmie, driven by his junior, thank goodness, around the crofts to see the bull, rams or stallion that he had sent over. I say thank goodness his junior was driving, because you HAD to take a dram at every croft, as if you didn't you would cause grave offence. But the thing I will never forget to my dying day was hearing the sound of the pipes not once, not twice, but three or more times that night. I heard that wonderful haunting lilting sound of the 'piob mhor' coming over the peat hags of Uist. I was a middling boy piper myself and I love the sound of them to this day – not (as all too often one hears them) at dinners, Burns Suppers etc., but as one hears them on the Esplanade of Edinburgh Castle when they play 'The Black Bear'. I'm in my late seventies now, but at that sound any recruiting sergeant could tap me on the shoulder and I'd be off to join the the Queens' Colours. Oh yes, the pipes have a lot to answer for when it comes to the magnificent record the Scottish Territorial Batallions have had in recruitment. In another chapter in this book you have read about Bob Maxwell, then my officer, who like me had played the pipes as a boy; and on that magical night that Jimmie Dean and I went around Uist hearing those lone pipers, I was moved to tears as I remembered Bob reciting the following to me as we lay under the African stars wondering if the next shell had our name on it:

As I walked under the African Moon,
I heard the piper play,
And the last time ever I heard the tune,
Was a thousand miles away.

Far to the West in a deep cut bay,
By the ceaseless sound of the sea,
We lived and laughed in a happier day,
Archie, Johnnie and me.

For they'd be piping half the night,
At every ceilidh by,
And I'd be dancing with all my might,
As long as they played would I.

Many a time we were at the games,
And many a prize had we,
And never a one but called our names,
Archie and Johnnie and Me.

But Archie's dead in the Libyan sand,
And Johnnie was left in Crete,
And I'm alone in a distant land,
With the music gone from my feet.

I heard him under the African Moon,
The piper I could not see,
Yet certain I am that he played that tune,
For Archie, Johnnie and Me.

Modern ferries have revolutionised the Islands but I sincerely hope they will be able to keep their wonderful identity and individuality that this country needs so badly today.

No way in a book of this sort would I go into arguments about the clearances, the crofting system and so on, but one thing I am willing to say is that crofting and farming a small farm is a way of life. I have been castigated a million times by the N.F.U., political gurus etc. who say farming is a business. That's O.K. if you're in Lincolnshire, Norfolk, Suffolk, East Yorkshire, East Lothian, Fife, parts of Aberdeenshire, the Black Isle (the daddy of them all for me) but not in the wetter areas. I could be wrong, and I've been so many times in my life, but I think farming in the less favoured areas will come back to those of us who love the way of life and are willing to forego the 'ritz' one can have if one has a large farm in a favoured area. When I wanted some more cash to educate my family I did a bit of broadcasting, factoring estates etc, and if one can't do that every farmer of a small place or his wife will have something they can do to augment their living. What has this to do with Jimmie Dean you say? Just a helluva lot, because he advised those crofters and small farmers on the sort of stock they ought to breed for the kind of land they were farming. I'm told by my farming pals that nowadays to make money in farming you have to know how to fill in the forms, not how to farm the land. God help us is all I can say.

Back in the fifties when I knew Jimmie best he was very interested in getting a stallion scheme going in the Shetland Islands for the Shetland Pony Society. I, at that time, hadn't been to Shetland but have since, and now realise why Jimmie held the breed in such high regard and wanted to improve them. When one sees the terrain on which the ponies run – bare acid-filled grazing with but the sparest of shelter – and yet many, in fact most of the mares, will foal for the first time at three years of age. There is no doubt the available seaweed helps tremendously with its supply of minerals. When I eventually went to Shetland and saw the ponies on their native heath with their big bellies I realised why they are so big. It is because they have to eat a lot of the available roughage to keep alive, hence the size. To see a Shetland pony mare on her home island, suckling and making a good job of her foal after wintering on the barest of 'keep', and without much or any shelter from those awful gales, fills me with admiration. As the late Robert Paterson of Burngrange, Weston, once said to me, 'When I see an old Blackfaced yow standing on a bare knowe in the end o' Mairch and obviously fu' o' lamb I tak' ma bunnet off to her'.

Yes, our native breeds have so many built in 'plusses' that it's sad that the urge to make more money has deflected many away from them. This also was the case with the Shetland Pony breed, as whenever Jimmie and the majority of the Shetland Pony Council decided a stallion scheme was needed to stop the use of anything being used as a stallion that had four legs and 'the two essentials', crofters started bumping up the mare numbers and of course over-grazed their ground and produced inferior stock. However, 'forty years on', although they are still having slight hiccups, the Shetland Pony Society have a stallion scheme which is the envy of many other pony societies.

During the period Jimmie was trying to help the Shetland crofters improve their ponies and their incomes, he was approached by someone in America to see if he would find them some miniature coloured horses (i.e. piebald, skewbald, chestnuts etc., not black which is the popular predominant colour nowadays) and export them. As a Department Official he couldn't do the job himself, but said if he found the ponies would I take them to Gaskbeg and arrange for them to be exported from Liverpool? As I needed every halfpenny I could make from that poor hill farm I jumped at the chance of an extra buck or two.

My daughter Sara and her friend Adrienne tell me that they had to herd them like sheep, and that they were into everyone's fields and gardens, as even at 1,000 feet above sea level Gaskbeg must have been the land of Goschen to them! I can't remember the minute details of the ponies (all twenty of them) coming to our farm, but they must have been tiny, as they all travelled to Liverpool in the farm's ex-army wartime Austin lorry with its home-made float, and they were certainly cheap because I know they cost £5 each delivered to Gaskbeg!!

But thank goodness things have changed for the Shetland Island pony breeders and the world demand is fantastic. Their ability to be driven, or ridden in events as unlikely as the 'Shetland Pony Grand National', have proven to the world that this breed which started its life as an essential part of a crofter's livelihood, then became famous as pit ponies, can now be part of this world-wide cult of being 'built in horse', as horses were never so popular. I like to think that you, my old pal Jimmie, helped the Shetland Ponies to get their share of this tremendous upsurge in the love and use of the horse.

I think when I was asked to judge the horse championship at Perth Show some years ago between the Clydesdale, the Highland and the Shetland, and gave the championship to the Shetland Pony mare, I heard Jimmie's voice in my ear saying, 'If you get a richt mover they're the best of the lot'. And she was a right mover and was the best of the lot that day. One of the problems in the Mountain and Moorland breeds today is that not enough breeders have had to use the breed for the purpose for which they were intended, and all too often they are not 'richt movers'.

The Highland Cattle Society too was helped by him. He needed bulls of that breed to go to the Islands to keep up the stock of Highland females, from which were bred the famous Cross Highland Cows which to this day are excellent hill cows. It was from them that the Luing Cattle were produced, although in my humble opinion they were never as hardy, because being in-bred they had lost that essential in all first crosses, hybrid vigour. Jimmie decided that post-war there were too many Highland Cattle being bred for 'hair and horn', so he started up a D.O.A.S. fold at Wester Aberchalder, Gorthlick. The hair and horn brigade were usually folds run by cattlemen who wanted to win at the major shows, and sadly they were the folds backed by considerable amounts of money and of course having won at shows they were the folds whose bulls made most at the annual Oban Bull Sales. I remember Jimmie telling me about a bull called 'Alasdair Ruaradh' from the Black Isle, bred and used by a Major Shaw MacKenzie. What a bull: head, flesh, right on his legs, plenty of bone, you name it he had it, and Jimmie tried to buy him for the D.O.A.S. fold but was stuck for cash (as is so usual in Government controlled operations!) I bought him for the late Lord Rootes, and his progeny have done well through the Muirheads of Corriemuchloch. But I always remember Jimmie moaning about his neighbour at Easter Aberchalder, a certain retired naval officer, Captain Bethell, and little did I realise that the Captain's adopted neice Sally, who was working there, was to be my wife!

Then we met later on, on the Aberdeen-Angus front. He was always so good at passing on bulls from Knocknagael (that were coming back on their daughters) to farmers where he thought they would some good. His Department bulls had the greatest testing ground in Scotland if not Britain, as at that time the cows they were serving were all well bred and so after a couple of years he knew which of his bulls was breeding well. I, among many other struggling young hill farmers, gained from the Department's 'cast offs'.

Because he had to buy so many bulls each year for the Department, Jimmie had entrée to every pedigree herd in Scotland and could get free drams the length and breadth of the country. He was also known by overseas buyers as a first class judge of stock. One American asked him to buy him an Aberdeen-Angus stock bull. Once again, as a Department official, Jim couldn't take on the commission but very kindly handed over the order to me. At that time the length and breadth of Speyside had herds of pedigree Aberdeen-Angus cattle (sadly no longer) so I was able to take the American to six different herds with bulls on offer. He chose a bull at the farm of a dear friend of mine called Bert Hendry, of Advie Mains, and after seeing the bull made him walk out again for the second time, after which we were asked into the house for the essential dram (actually nearly a tumblerful of pure malt). My American friend said 'I'm interested in your bull, Mr. Hendry, but what's his price?' Whereupon Bert stated a figure that I thought was about double the bull's value and made me splutter into my glass. 'Done,' said the Yank without a moment's hesitation, and Bert, realising the Yank would have gone higher, said, 'Don't forget we deal in guineas in pedigree cattle in Scotland, not pounds'. Quick thinking, Bert.

Then there was that great friend of Jimmie's who was a Sergeant in the 'Polis' in Speyside. Everyone wondered why he was never promoted, but I was one of the few that knew he didn't want promotion, and why? Sergeant X was the best connoisseur of whisky it had been my pleasure to know. Part of his duties was to check the distilleries in Speyside for theft, illegal trafficking and oh! just any old excuse for his entry. Like all old time 'Bobbies' he was a jovial character and was made welcome wherever he went. All distilleries dispensed free drams to every visitor in those days, and it was the real McKay too, clear stuff. As we used to say, 'If my mother had milk like this I would ne'er have been speaned'. The old Sergeant realised that he would be offered much more than he could consume, so craftily he had a copper container made to fit onto his belt, so fashioned that it didn't show through his tunic. There was a wee stopper on the top and it held much more than the Distillery managers realised!! No wonder the Sergeant didn't want promotion. When I asked him once why he didn't want it he said, 'Ben, I'm very happy here'! I think many a leading businessman in London would have swopped jobs with him. Living in that wonderful Strath, mixing with some of the friendliest people it has been my pleasure to know, with some of the best sporting opportunities in Britain at your door, including, in the Spey, one of the top salmon-fishing rivers in Britain. Then, to top all of that, enough free malt whisky for the rest of your life!!

I often wonder what happened to the Sergeant's whisky. I well remember Jimmie and I sitting in his room, and he had arrayed in front of us between a dozen and twenty Speyside malts. We were asked to tell which was which. Jimmie, born and bred on Speyside, knew a few, but I who have never been a good taster (my love of the malts in these days was 'the notions it put in my heid'), didn't do too well. But over the years I have no doubts that Smith's (George and J.G.) Glenlivet is the daddy of them all (and I'm not being paid for a commercial as I don't know them). I love Highland Park from Orkney, which I'd put second, and Glenmorangie, also from Speyside, third (or perhaps Macallan, Glenlivet).

I'm thrilled for areas like Speyside that there is worldwide recognition of the clean drink that is whisky. Every country has its own tipple, and if you've ever stalked a stag or hind at 2,000 feet above sea level, or gathered sheep from the tops in a 'snell' east wind with snow in the air, thrown a curling stone at an outside Bonspiel, or finished dancing a 'Broon's Reel' you will realise why whisky is the drink for Scotland! Back in the fifties when I knew Jimmie, although Speyside was full of distilleries the export side was as nothing compared with today. In those days the reason Jimmie and I knew so much about the distilleries (apart from our love of their products) was that they all owned good herds of cattle, as draff, which is the reject husks of the barley from which the whisky is distilled, is excellent cattle feed. They produced excellent cattle and also excellent cattlemen. Sandy Gray was one of the best cattlemen I was honoured to work with, and he started life at a distillery, as did Robbie McHardy who appears in this book.

Whisky is big business for the Highlands today, and Whisky Trails are numerous–and what better to do on a dreich Scottish summer's day, of which we have all too many. Even H.R.H. the Prince of Wales has given his blessing to malt whisky by allowing 'Laphroaig' to have his Royal assent.

For me the West Coast malts are too 'peaty', but 'chacun à son goût', and thereby hangs a tale. Back in the seventies the Aberdeen-Angus Society sent a mission to the Argentine, and as Chief Executive I was told I was in charge. We had in the party a super guy, one Gerry Rankin, partly because he was the best judge of a cattle beast it's been my pleasure to know, but also because he'd been in the Argentine pre-war and was a passable interpreter. When we got to Buenos Aires we were taken to our hotels but told not to expect to buy whisky, as it was £36 per bottle!

Total chaos ensued until Gerry turned up with a CASE of 'Chivas Regal' donated by a great Anglophile Argentinian, one Charlie Duggan. Gerry, who is himself a gin drinker, said to my room mate, 'You'd better taste it as it cost the donor over £40 a bottle'. The said gentleman swilled it round his mouth and said slowly, 'It's a bit peaty'!!! I could have murdered him. Talk about looking gift horses in the mouth!

The last time I was with Jimmie was at a Perth Bull Sale when they were held in the old Mart in Caledonian Road, Perth. He and his 'lieutenants', and they were a super gang, were ensconced in the Lounge of the Waverley Hotel with their sale catalogues checking which bulls they had bought, how much money they had spent, where each bull should go etc., etc. Oh, yes! they had a dram in their hands, but they had stood all day in a draughty ringside choosing carefully what they would buy, at the right price, and damned little thanks they would get for their shrewdness now when you think of the way some spend public money today.

I fear that years of chain-smoking, standing all day in freezing conditions at marts up and down the country, not eating regularly, maybe having the extra dram or two too many, but mainly not getting enough exercise, took this 'Auld Acquaintance' from us all too early. But although he never got a 'gong', Jimmie, as Chief Livestock Inspector, D.O.A.S., North of Scotland, would have done more for livestock in that area than many of the so-called 'master stocksmen' who got the honours and feathered their own nests!

SIR ARCHIBALD HECTOR McINDOE K.B.E., F.R.C.S.

Famous plastic surgeon and benefactor to many, especially the author

Archie will be the only character of whom I write who was not born in Scotland. But I reckon if Sean Lineen, with his New Zealand accent and birth, can play rugby for Scotland, then Archie, whose parents emigrated from Scotland to New Zealand can appear as a 'Scots Character'.

When I was brought back to the mouth of the Clyde, after being wounded, then torpedoed, and having spent all too many days on a raft in the area of the Equator, it was just marvellous to see the hills of Argyll, as it was late November, all snow capped. Little did I think that some of the hills I was looking at would be connected to my future life. Bute, which I saw to the west, was the island from where Archie's parents emigrated, and to the north were the hills around the estates I was to manage in the sixties and seventies. What a magnificent sight they all were, especially to those of us who had come home from the 'Burning Sands of Egypt'.

I am always sorry for those who have no faith and think things just happen by accident. No one is going to tell me that my getting the benefit of Archie's surgical skill and even more of his shrewd advice was just a coincidence. The first thing that led to it was Eric Dalling, the Dental Surgeon of the Maxillo-Facial team in No.8 General Hospital, Alexandria, telling me that by hook or by crook I was to get to East Grinstead to be seen by the up-and-coming surgeon McIndoe. The second thing nobody could have predicted. Who was to know that I was to be torpedoed and that my medical records would finish up feeding the fishes? Which allowed me to tell the Medical Board at Buchanan Castle Hospital that had they seen my records they would have seen that I was due to go to East Grinstead. What a lie that was (forgive me, oh Lord!) as Archie was the Plastic Surgeon for the Royal Air Force, not the Army. Their plastic surgeons were at Basingstoke in England, or at Broxburn in Scotland. The third thing was that after the Board had inspected where my nose had been (not a pretty sight, as sadly, though the team in Alexandria had done their best, according to Archie they had made it not much better after ten operations), they conceded the point to the extent of contacting Queen Victoria Hospital, East Grinstead, by phone.

At that time things there were fairly basic and the famous Ward Three was a Nissen Hut stuck onto the side of a typically pretty country cottage hospital. The operating theatres were in the main building – now there are beautiful new ones in the new wings.

Believe it or not Archie was checking something out at the entrance desk when the phone call came through from Scotland, and the girl said, 'It's for you'. When he asked what the 'Brown' job wanted doing, the doctor in Scotland said, 'He needs half a new face and a new nose'. To which the great man replied, 'I haven't done a nose for a bit, send him on down.' So began firstly an acquaintanceship and latterly a friendship that continued until his far too early death, all of forty years ago.

What fun we had in old Ward Three in those early days. It was full of ex-Battle of Britain pilots, many of them now household names. Richard Hillary, author of *The Last Enemy*. Tom Gleeve, the chief Guinea Pig, who sadly passed away this year, and with whom I had friendly arguments as to whose Rhinoplastic nose was the best! Bill Simpson who wrote two wartime best-sellers. Geoff Page, an especial friend of the Maestro's, who was adviser to Nigel Havers' excellent film *The Perfect Hero* and also the instigator of the Battle of Britain War Memorial at Dover which the Queen Mother unveiled last summer. Paul Hart, who made such a success of bulb-growing and helped Archie in the latter's Kenyan farm. The list is endless, but all those above accepted me as an equal – which could not be said for some of the others, who resented my being there at all, and even more that the great man often took me along with Geoff and one Robin Johnston to his house or some of the parties to which he had been invited.

Our 'local' was not really a pub at all, but rather the centre of operations for 'Letheby and Christopher's', the caterers for most of the top social events pre-war such as Ascot, Henley etc., etc. Because of their contacts their ration of alcoholic beverages was way above that of the normal local pubs, as all licensed premises during the war got a percentage of what they had sold pre-war. But that wasn't the only reason that we used the Whitehall. The manager there, one Bill Gardiner, was a rather special 'mine host': Archie got to know him and knew he could trust him. Between them they organised mirrors around the bar so that we got used to our scars, flaps, pedicles, Rhinoplasts etc., etc. Mine were as nothing compared with the burns cases, and one only had to see them (and hear them in the saline baths getting their dressing removed) to realise what pain they used to bear.

Sir Archibald McIndoe

The one and only Archie McIndoe, a.k.a. Sir Archibald Hector McIndoe, the famous wartime plastic surgeon and one of three people who influenced the author's life. 'The Boss' to the Guinea Pig Club that he formed, but greatly missed adviser and friend to the author

Also, Archie got Bill to keep an eye on any of us who, usually because of stress, was taking too much 'grog'. Drinking before an operation was, of course, not on, and in any normal hospital one wouldn't have been allowed out for days before one: but because of the number of operations most of us required (and my twenty five was as nothing compared to most of the burns cases) Archie put us on our honour to play the game, and with but few exceptions his method worked. Although I do remember the occasion, after he was given his wonderful new operating theatre which was complete with a visitors' gallery, and all those from Ward Three not 'for the chop' were invited to see the great man perform an operation on one of our pals. Blood spurted everywhere, and Archie looked up to us and said, 'Now you see why I don't want you to drink for days before your next operation – if you do you'll bleed like an ordinary pig, not just a Guinea Pig!'

'The Boss', as we called him, was always thinking about anything that would take our minds off our wounds and the dreary round of day-to-day hospital routine. He was a great man for publicity and was way before his time. The old guard of a committee who ran the Cottage Hospital pre-war were not at all amused that this upstart of a 'colonial' should invite the Press, film stars, music hall personalities, you name them – if they brought publicity to the Hospital, Archie used them. One of the first things he had done was to 'vet' the V.A.D.'s (the Auxiliary Nurses) who wanted to join the team at East Grinstead, and the result was we had a lot of girls who were 'smashers'. Some of them married some of the patients, as the 'mothering' instinct seems very strong in some females and they felt they could help the burnt or wounded person, sadly not always with success.

Archie was very attractive to the opposite sex and as his marriage was a rocky one, with as always faults on both sides, he was constantly being invited out to different parties. While his marriage was slowly falling apart he was more than kind to me, as he felt it was too bad to ask me to go back to Scotland between each operation.

I remember vividly two occasions when Archie had me to stay at his flat in London. He was still doing quite a bit of work in Harley Street and as he was to be away all morning he asked me to go and get some fish for supper, for which, as for all foodstuffs that were scarce during the war, one had to queue. He gave me rather intricate directions as to where I'd find the queue. When I joined it the people didn't seem the sort with whom an eminent surgeon would mix, but it being war time we were 'a' Jock Tamson's Bairns' and social barriers were largely broken down. After standing for five minutes I realised that those who were coming away from the front didn't seem to be carrying anything resembling fish, so I said to the toothless old crone in front of me, 'Is this the fish queue?' Back came the reply, 'No, it's for spirits, my dear'. I was in the 'Meths' queue! Then there was the great occasion when the 'Boss' took me to

Harrods. All I knew of Harrods until that great day had been gleaned from a stud hand who worked for the then Chairman of the store, who owned a thoroughbred stud farm not far from the stud on which I was employed pre-war. This groom had visited the famous store and was full of praise of its marvellous food-hall (in which I have since spent far too much money!)

The day I went with Archie he was looking for a new piano, of all things. I questioned him why he was using Harrods and not a recognised piano shop, and he pointed out that Harrods had a better selection during the war than any music shop. Archie always enjoyed 'tinkling the ivories', and many a happy evening he gave us as we all relaxed at 'Little Warren', his wee cottage at East Grinstead. On that day at Harrods he seemed to have every attendant in the store buzzing round him like bees, as he was already famous.

I can't remember after all these years whether he actually bought a piano that day, but I do remember him telling me what a thrill it had been to try out so many expensive pianos by famous makers and to be recognised by so many people!

Plastic surgery needs long breaks in between operations, and so it was that the great man organised my discharge from the Army with the famous line, 'this man is needed by the Agricultural Industry and I predict he will make a name for himself' (you could have fooled me). But I suppose now that I've done forty-seven years of broadcasting on farming matters, some T.V. farming appearances, judging at most of the major shows and acting as Agricultural Adviser to a T.V. show, 'Strathblair' he must have been right! So he arranged my discharge, and I was lucky enough to get a Farm Manager's job in my beloved Strathearn where I have spent much of my life. But although I was discharged from the Army I had to have quite a few operations to complete my new nose to the Maestro's' satisfaction. I remember returning for one such operation when a few of my old pals were in Ward Three. Archie wasn't too busy and had a well known war time reporter, one Godfrey Wynn, staying with him. As I've said he never lost a trick when it came to publicity, and he asked us from the Ward to join them for a meal so that Godfrey could get our views about the Hospital and make up his story. I think I've said that the famous Ward Three was an ancient Nissen Hut, and it had an old coke-burning stove in the centre which ate coke and even when red hot, and it often was, it only gave out heat about a yard away.

Anyway, on this particular night when we all got back to the Ward Godfrey asked would Archie take him there so that he could get a feel of the atmosphere. Can you imagine any other hospital in the country allowing a reporter, no matter how well known, and Godfrey certainly was, into a ward at eleven at night? We were standing in a ring round the stove. As usual when I got back to civvy street I was wearing the kilt, and this wee chap said, 'I do love you raw boned Scots'. Whereupon Archie quipped, 'Look out, Ben, don't go to bed too soon or you might have company'. Complete collapse of the 'Guinea Pigs' and embarrassment of our visitor, whom I didn't know had a fondness for his own sex. Godfrey Wynn was not only a brilliant reporter but a very brave man. He went in a destroyer on the infamous Murmansk trip to Russia through those terrifying frozen Northern waters not just once but twice!

Another time I went South for an operation and stayed with Archie, and it must have been in 1945, as brother Frank was captaining the Army rugger team that year. Frank had got me tickets for the Army versus R.A.F. match at Twickenham and I got the great man to join me.

I remember two things about that match, which was disappointing with far too many scrums. The first was that Frank, although a good kicker himself, gave someone else the penalties and conversions which the other fellow kept missing. So right at the end of the match, when the Army were getting beaten, Frank took over and won the match with a magnificent kick from the touchline. In the tearoom after the game one of the Army chiefs, most of whom, as well as all the top brass R.A.F., knew the 'Boss', said to Archie (who of course was shouting for the R.A.F.) 'If Coutts had only taken over the kicking from the start of the match we'd have beaten you by an even bigger margin, but he's too modest'. And Archie replied, 'It runs in the family'. Bless you my old friend.

On the way home after the match he said what a rotten game it had been, and added: 'Wait till the Kiwis come over after the war and they'll show you all what rugby is all about'. Prophetic words indeed.

After I had been discharged from the Army I was more than lucky to get a farm manager's job, although my pre-war experience in farming was as a farm worker. Fortunately Sir James Roberts who employed me had an extremely efficient office system run by an extremely efficient secretary, Molly Walker. This allowed his farm managers to concentrate on practical farming. Oh, how things have changed – with knowledge of computers now an essential for any farm or estate manager and also a complete knowledge of filling in forms. I saw in a farming paper in early 1994 that some poor lad had filled in his boss's forms incorrectly and had lost the estate tens of thousands of pounds. You can thank your lucky stars I didn't have your forms to fill in, Jim! In hindsight probably one of the reasons why I got that manager's job, which set me off on a not too unsuccessful farming career, was because the farm manager had to stay in a very large house. Lawhill was built as a shooting lodge for the northern part of Strathallan Estate, and as a result had big rooms not easily furnished by the usual farm manager. It also had the most fantastic view across Strathearn to the Ochil Hills. My wife Creina was a wartime widow, her husband having been one of those brave amateur sailors who took their small craft to help the evacuation of Dunkirk and didn't come back. Sad we hear so little of these heroes today. Because of her previous marriage Creina had some nice furniture, although not enough to fill a shooting lodge!

When Archie heard I had got settled into my first post-war job, and my goodness how many of us who came under his care have to thank him for our lives and livelihoods ever since, he said he'd like to come to visit. I knew he'd always been keen on the odd day's shooting so told him to come in winter when the geese came into Strathearn, then in their hundreds, now in their thousands.

Strange how patterns of wildlife have changed in my lifetime. Lawhill, for instance, was built as a shooting lodge because the partridge shooting was famous pre-war. Then we had acres of turnips, lots of cover and we didn't know what sprays were. Now there are practically no 'neeps', everything is sprayed, which kills all the wee beasties on which the partridges feed, and one would be lucky to see more than one covey where once one used to see dozens. Geese on the other hand have multiplied. In my days at Lawhill the geese came in from the saltings to graze but flew out at night. Now they come into Strathearn in their thousands and winter there, going to one of three lochs to preen themselves, Ochtertyre, Carsebreck or Dupplin. When Archie came up to stay it was hopeless from a goose shooting point of view as it was frosty and windless and the geese were far too high.

His notes in my visitors' book read 'Second Footman, Lawhill, food good, geese no good. Work too hard but best job in Perthshire'. Luckily Fisher Ferguson, of whom you will read elsewhere in this book, invited us up to Glenartney to shoot white hares. We had a lovely day with snow on the tops and hard, hard frost, and the 'Boss' really enjoyed himself, but he realised sitting on a surgeon's stool is not the way to get fit for walking Scottish hills!

Among the many things for which I have to thank him is that before he came, and knowing he liked a 'night cap', I had scoured the local grocers to procure 'a wee dram' for the great man. The sum total of my effort was a half bottle of gut rot. I knew Sir James Roberts drank something that was rather special because when we went curling together he always had a flask, and was more than lavish in how he dispensed it in those drink-scarce days. So I went to Jim and asked if he could help. Thus started my happy association with Matthew Gloag's 'Famous Grouse' whisky, of which in 1945 I and many others had never heard, but which now is a household name. Jim told me to go into Bordeaux House in Perth telling the storeman (luckily an ex-serviceman) that I was his manager and could he help me? I must say I thought I'd be lucky to get a bottle, even for the great man, but when the storeman said 'Will half a dozen bottles do?' they nearly had to call an ambulance for me.

'Cast your bread upon the waters' the good book says. Archie got Grouse whisky into the College of Surgeons bar. I got it into the Farmer's Club in London. In all the overseas countries I visited for the Aberdeen-Angus Society, as I always wore my kilt I was asked which blend of whisky I drank, and the answer was always the same.

By 1945 Archie was a household name as were his 'Guinea Pigs' so it was natural that he personally knew and was known by all the landlords and grandees around East Grinstead. The Dewar family, who make their money from blending 'White Label' whisky in Perthshire, not only owned the Dupplin Estate in that county but also an estate in Sussex near East Grinstead. So when Archie came to stay with me he said, 'I must phone my friend John Dewar'. The result of that call was that Archie, Geoff Page, who had come north with him, and I were invited to Dupplin for a day's rough shooting. I can't remember what, after forty-nine years, we shot, but I'll never forget the lunch. As I've said earlier whisky was hard to come by but when mine host asked Geoff what he would like to drink he said, 'A beer, please'. Archie and I said, 'Whisky, please', being in the house of Dewar, and not only were we allowed to help ourselves from a lovely decanter, from memory it was 'Ancestor', one of their special blends. During lunch the butler/houseman came in and said that our host was wanted on the phone, which in those days was always situated in the hall. No sooner was the door closed than Geoff moved faster than he did in his fighter plane to win his D.S.O. and D.F.C. to grab the whisky, and by the time our host came back there was precious little left in the decanter!

I was more than proud that Archie did us the honour of visiting us at Lawhill as he had so many prestigious friends, but like all exiled Scots he had a yearning to return to the land of his 'ain folk'. When I motor south now on our motorway system I realise what a long journey it must have been for him and Geoff in Archie's Rolls Royce, which had been moth-balled for the duration. O.K., there was no traffic, but one had to go through every town from London to Perth.

Archie asked me in 1952 to manage a farm for him in Kenya, but as I was in a steady job, Creina and I decided to stay put. Oh! how many who came through his surgical hands have him to thank for the jobs they got after the war. To instance but one there was a glorious gallus fellow-Scot called Jock Tosh who was set up by the 'Boss', who was always getting backers like Marks and Spencer's to help his Guinea Pigs to get a start in civvy street. Dear old Jock 'pranged' not one, but three coal lorries (with the drink taken), but Archie had infinite patience with us, although not with his operating team, to whom he could be pretty vicious if they handed him the wrong scalpel!

Archie, now free from marital ties, found that Kenya was the place to go to recharge his batteries. Robin Johnston, whom I've mentioned before as one of Archie's close friends along with Geoff Page, Paul Hart and myself, was involved with this. As Robin pre-war had been a District Commissioner in Tanganyika he helped Archie buy a farm on Kilimanjaro which gave the Maestro immense pleasure, but I would guess not a lot of profit as there were then six thousand elephants in that district, and if only a few descended on your crops, bang went the profit in one night. During his stay there Paul, who had farmed in Lincolnshire, used to go with him, and he tells how they originally went in an Argonaut plane which made six stops en route! Changed days indeed. Paul also speaks about Archie's tie-up with Michael Woods, later to be Sir Michael Woods, whose widow Sue is doing such a super job in Kenya to this day. Michael had the contacts and Archie the know-how, and if the farm needed a new tractor the 'Maestro' had to do a day's operating, which meant eight operations, but if the need was for a combine then he had to do at least two days' operating! Thank goodness you're not having to do operations for a new combine nowadays, my old pal – you'd never be on them (which I know you loved to be), because it would cost you weeks of operating!

In 1953, by which time Paul and Mike Woods had bought the neighbouring farm to Archie's, things were going nicely for them. They used to go off to parties around the other side of Kilimanjaro, which took them a day there and a day back, and of course they always stayed the night. Archie was fancy free, Kenya really recharged his batteries, and he was blessed with a skin that turned mahogany in the sun.

He had always said to Paul how blissful it was not to have a telephone and to have the nearest Post Office twenty miles away, but in 1953 to 1954 he started saying to Robin and Paul, 'Don't you think we ought to visit the Baron?' This was a foreigner of whom up to then Archie had not been too fond, but who stayed near the Post Office. Or he would say 'Poor old Brownie' (the person who ran the Post Office) 'I'll bet he's a bit lonely, shouldn't we take him some gin?' Whereupon Robin said to Paul, 'There must be a bird that really matters if the Boss wants the mail'. And sure enough there was. Paul was sent back by the Kenyan partners to look her over, and as he said to me forty years later, 'Ben, she was a show stopper'. Connie Belcham was and still is (as Connie McIndoe) forty years on. Sadly they had such a short time together, but I remember well Connie with her immaculate taste getting Archie out of Little Warren into a super house in Forest Row. They very kindly had me to stay, and while Connie was cooking and the Boss and I were reminiscing he said, 'Well, what's the verdict?' and I replied, 'For my book she'd win any female championship if I were the judge'. Connie has done a wonderful job since Archie died in the Blond McIndoe Research Programme, the Marsden Hospital and many other charities, and I'm only sad that they didn't have more years together.

Archie, I left you to be the last of my characters because of all fourteen you have had the greatest lasting influence on my life. How could I possibly imagine, having been a mere groom and farm worker pre-war that when you said 'I predict he will make a name for himself in Agriculture' I should finish up with an M.B.E. for services to Agriculture and be made a Fellow of the Agriculture Societies?

Bless you my dear friend, what a lot you did for us who were lucky enough to come under your surgical skill, and to me, more importantly, your psychology, all that half century ago.

I thought of you when I was asked to open a new restaurant in Perth where I was written up as 'the well known veteran farmer, broadcaster and author'. Believe it or not the owners were Letheby and Christopher from East Grinstead, the owners of the 'Whitehall'. Boy, could I have told the assembled company about the times we had there. Just thanks for everything. I've tried to do the best I could, because you always said, 'Nothing but the best for me'.